Such Fragile Futures

An Artist and a Poet Reflect in a Garden

For Cheryl,
with warm wishes,
Brigid Collins

Brigid Collins
Christine De Luca

Christine De Luca

Main Point
BOOKS

First published 2025

ISBN: 978-1-7395214-8-6

This book is printed on FSC-certified paper
in a printing house that uses 100%
renewably-sourced energy

Printed and bound by
Totem Printing House

Typeset in Adobe Garamond by
Main Point Books, Edinburgh
www.mainpointbooks.co.uk

Contents

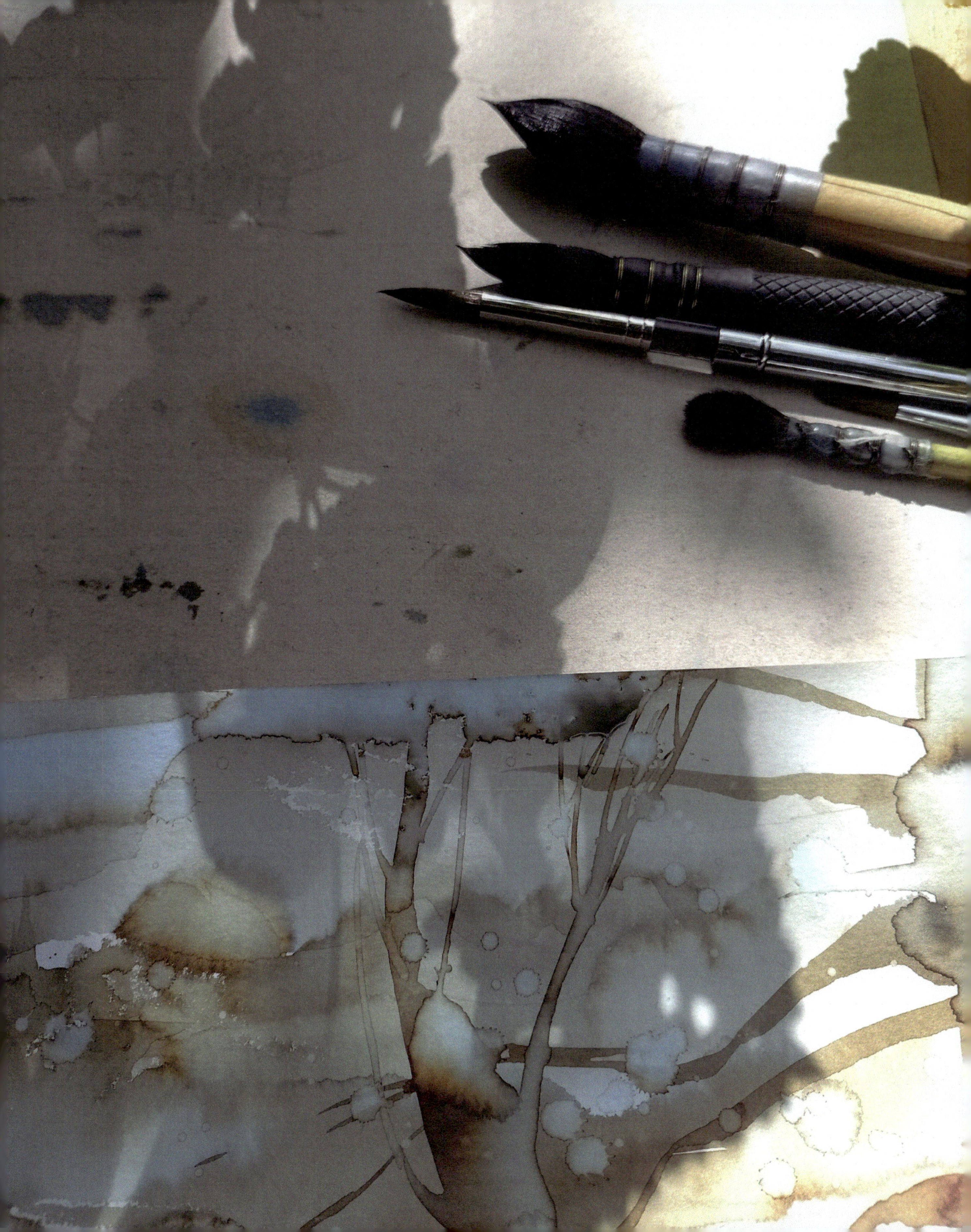

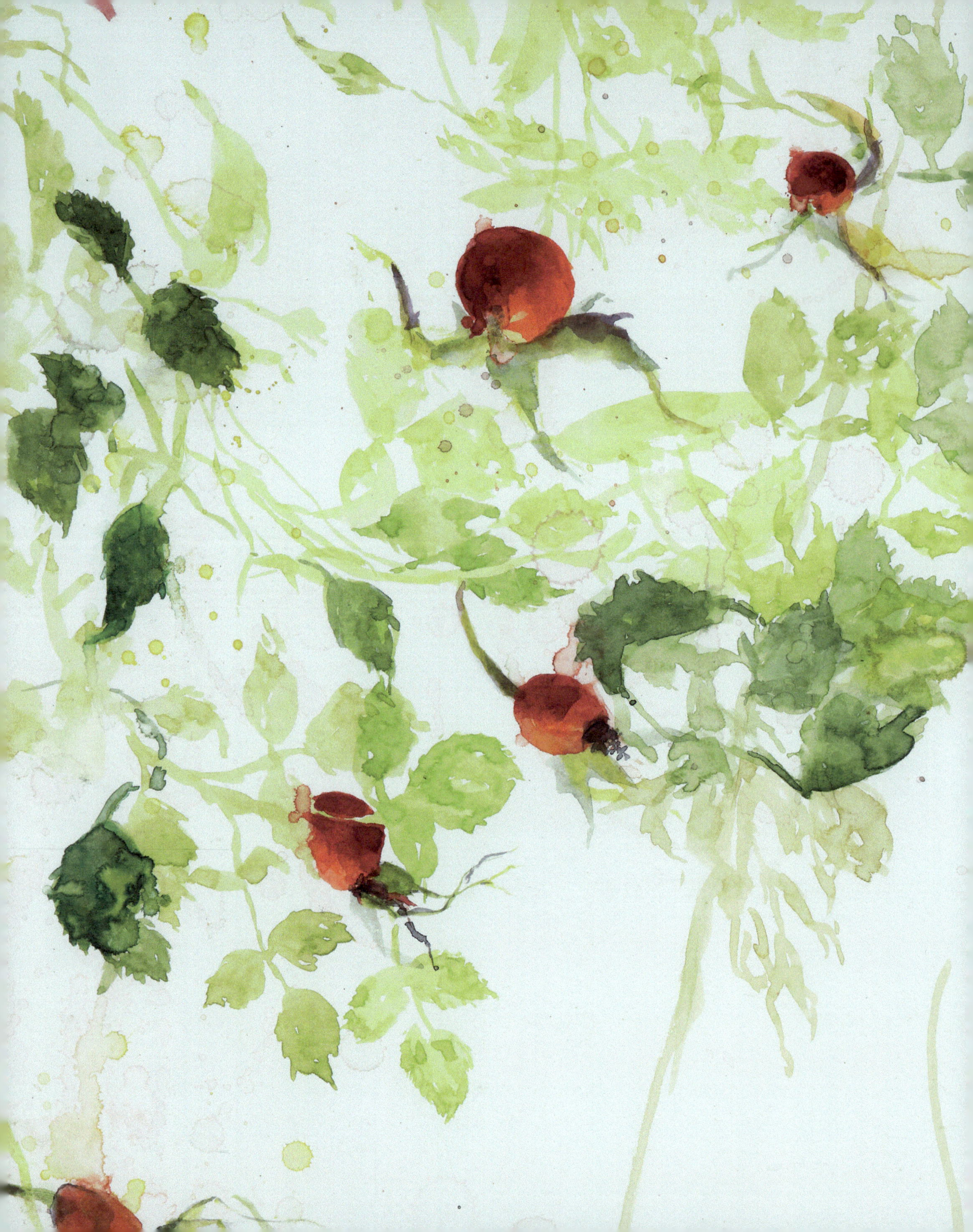

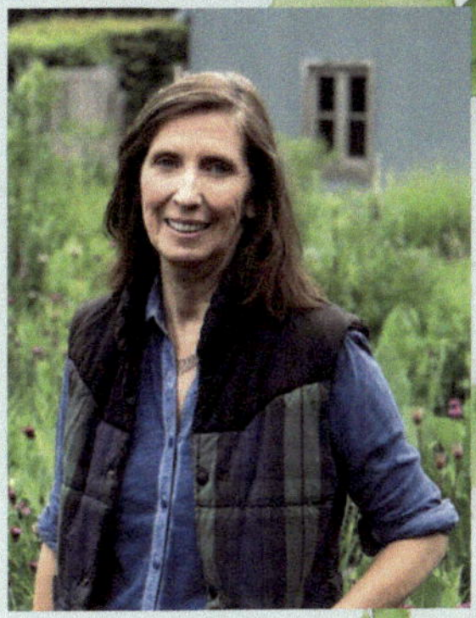

Foreword

Dr Sue Stuart-Smith
Author of *The Well Gardened Mind: Rediscovering Nature in the Modern World*

"...it is the quality of attention we pay and the sense of connectedness we feel, that makes the most difference. Yet so many aspects of contemporary life interfere with our capacity to slip into this mode of relaxed but close attention."

A garden is much more than a physical space, it is also a mental space. The feeling of safe enclosure and immersion in nature frees us from everyday pressures and gives us a sense of quiet so we can hear our own thoughts. Gardens can provide a meeting place for our innermost, dream-infused selves and the real world. They are where the wild and cultivated overlap, where we can lose ourselves and feel at one with nature around us. This sense of the 'in-between' is fundamental to how gardens encourage us to engage creatively with the natural world.

Dr Neil's garden exemplifies this quality of in-between space in a powerful way with its high wall on three sides and Duddingston loch on the other. The city centre is surprisingly close, yet this is a world apart. Surrounded by majestic hills, in close proximity to the ancient Kirk, it is a place in which light plays on water and the blue of the sky and greenness of the plants are somehow intensified so that our senses feel heightened, whilst the stones, trees, and meandering paths ground us and offer a physical and emotional resting place.

When Andrew and Nancy Neil set out to create this oasis of calm for their patients in the 1960's, they were drawing on a long tradition of healing gardens, though within their profession they were well ahead of their time, for it is only more recently that scientific research has confirmed the value of gardening and nature connection within healthcare. Research shows that crucially, it is the quality of attention we pay and the sense of connectedness we feel, that makes the most difference. Yet so many aspects of contemporary life interfere with our capacity to slip into this mode of relaxed but close attention.

The combined effects of city living and modern technology have led to a devaluing of the slower rhythms of natural time, but in a garden, the pace of life is the pace of plants and if we allow ourselves we can slip into slow time and experience the world from a different perspective.

This is what the artist, Brigid Collins, and the poet, Christine De Luca set out to do in their year of wonder and exploration in the garden. The results can now be shared in this beautiful book. Their work transports us to a different mode of being through which we can feel part of something much larger than ourselves.

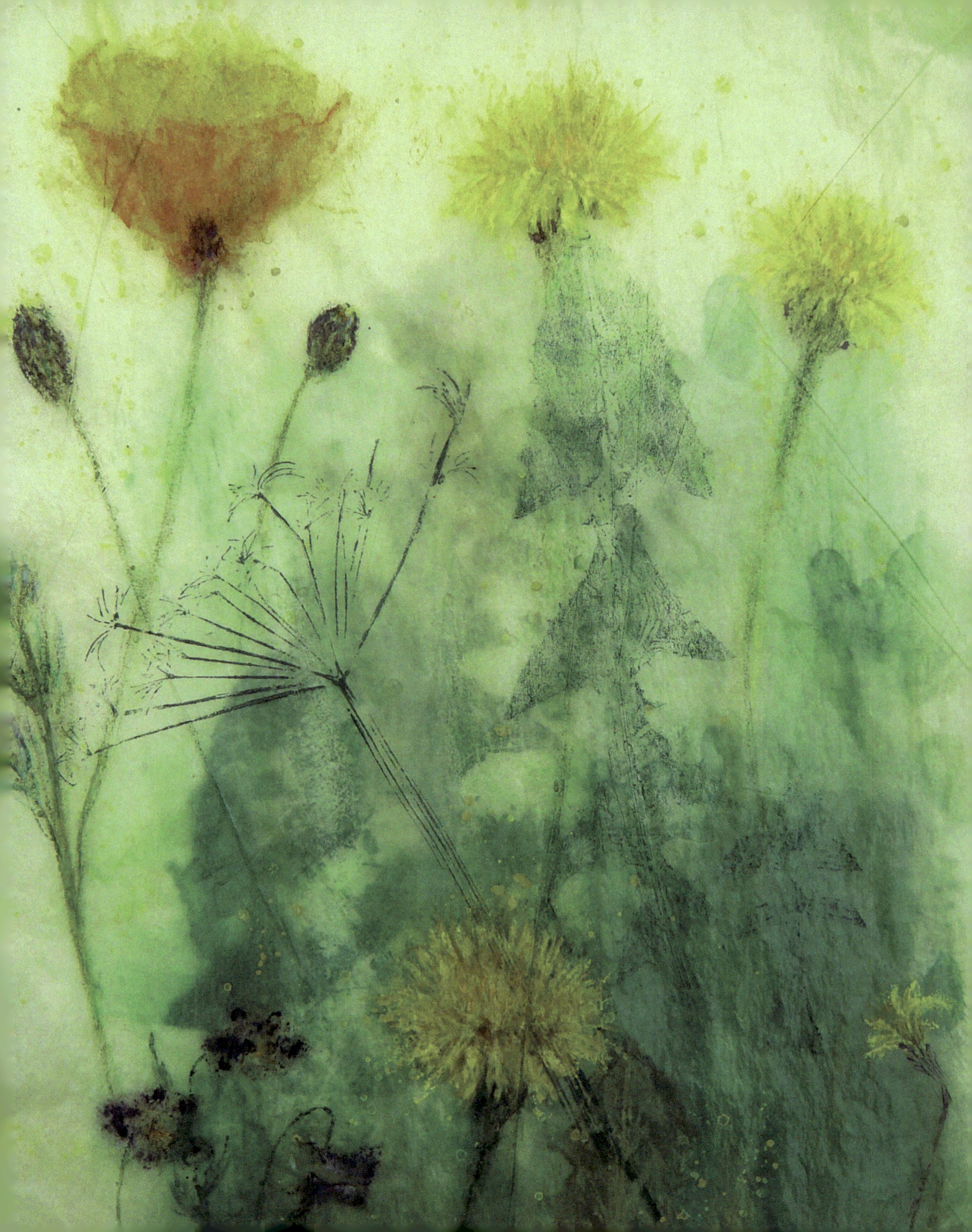

Introduction: The Story of a Collaboration between an Artist, a Poet and a Garden

Brigid Collins and Christine De Luca

"The world is not here
for us alone..."

Helen Macdonald in Vesper Flights

It was high summer when we began working together in Dr Neil's Garden in Duddingston, Edinburgh, where Brigid was Artist in Residence.

Reflecting on our time spent in the garden, we began to sense that our collaborative efforts were greater than the sum of the constituent parts – the art and the poetry – and that, alongside the growth that we were witnessing in the garden, a deepening of our mutual engagement with the natural world was underway. At that time, we had no particular intention of exploring spiritual matters in the context of the garden. But neither was our intention just to create either art that was conventionally botanical or poetry that was descriptive.

Discovering that our collaboration had a contemplative dimension, we began to realise that we could, perhaps, create something that might be helpful for others by sharing what we were experiencing there: a dusting off of the eyes which was allowing us to see more deeply and to notice in ourselves a burgeoning felt sense of what could be viewed as being a spiritual and psychological as much as a physical reality.

American poet Stanley Kunitz understood how the totality of a garden becomes formed in your mind as you move through it; in much the same way as you have to create the wholeness of a poem in your mind, by means of a process involving time spent in its company. We were both more than willing to give time to this process.

Many writers have commented on the joys of taking time to become intimate with a garden. Rowan Williams, exploring the nature of epiphany in a lecture on the visual arts, suggested:

"Art has a lot to do with time-taking for humans; we grow into our seeing. Epiphany is about acquiring habits of seeing differently, of taking time. It is not a lightning raid on the world but something to probe."

Rowan Williams, at New College Festival of Books and Religion (2022)

'Of all the communities we and wildlife find ourselves members of, the garden is one of the most intimate' writes *The Guardian*'s Nature Diary columnist Paul Evans, in his book *How To See Nature*.

"The most precious gift we can offer is our attention."

Thich Nhat Hanh, Buddhist monk

"Attention is the beginning of devotion."

Mary Oliver, poet

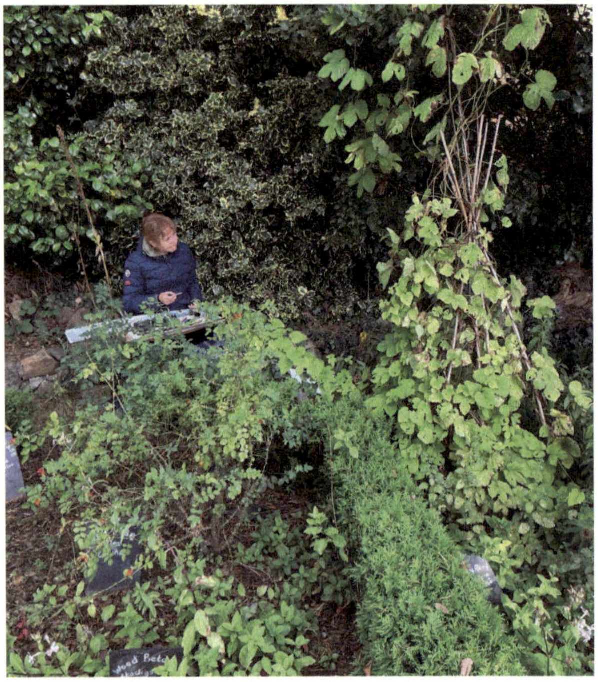

We began by simply spending time in the garden, often together, looking and learning, paying close attention. As artist, Brigid spent many hours – in all weathers – drawing and painting *en plein air*, then sharing her work with Christine. Occasionally a poem of Christine's would inspire Brigid to paint a particular plant but, more often, the visual work appeared to be acting as a stimulus for the poems. Such is the nature of ekphrasis. (An ekphrastic poem is, according to The Poetry Foundation, a vivid description of a scene or, more commonly, a work of art.)

We each sensed a deepening of our consciousness as, often in surprising ways, our fascination expanded rapidly: for example, our appreciation of how plants thrive best; of the complex harmonies in the natural world as symbiotic relationships; of the arbitrary designation of 'weeds'; of the incomer and of making room for the non-indigenous; of animal, vegetable, mineral and fungal harmony; of birds and other species as an integral part of the garden; of wonder; of peace; of the nature of beauty through the seasons of life; of nature as consoler and inspirator in difficult times; of the power of symbols to stir spiritual response; of the macrocosm being reflected in the microcosm; and, eventually, of an emerging sense of wholeness. We both began, simultaneously, to sense these shifts in awareness, sometimes almost imperceptibly, sometimes with a feeling of immensity. It was a time of learning and consequently of an increased appreciation of the natural world, and the place of humankind within it.

What follows here is therefore not just a series of drawings, paintings and poems expressing a range of ideas explored, but also our expression of a deep sense of gratitude, of hope and of love.

> "Our only hope of saving our planet is if we begin to have different feelings about it: perhaps if we became re-enchanted by the amazing improbability of life; perhaps if we suffered regret and even shame at what we've already lost; perhaps if we felt exhilarated by the challenges we face and what might yet become possible… we need to fall in love again, but this time with Nature."
>
> *Brian Eno (2022)*

Although coming from different disciplines, we found ourselves also able to share our particular perspectives. For example Christine observed:

> Deeply focused as we were on what was all around us and insulated, for a short while, from the incessant barrage of news and views, perhaps what we experienced there were momentary states of grace – states akin to what the poet, William Wordsworth described as being 'spots of time':

small, but memorable events, occurring mainly outdoors and when one is in touch with nature. These 'spots' have a lasting quality, according to Wordsworth, capable of 'lifting us up when we are fallen'. Such states connect us to our own essential nature, feel transformative and, by kindling a spirit of care and commitment for the whole planet, can lead towards an awareness of the interdependence of all things.

And Brigid observed:

> Our understanding of the interconnection between love of the natural world, of which we are a part, mixed with the wonder of it and the inspiration of art with what is numinous seemed to grow in this place, moment by moment.

"Whether imagined or real, gardens as refuges signify peace, comfort, freedom and hope, and are sites of pleasure, contentment, spirituality and sanity."

Where birds felt louder: The garden as a refuge during COVID-19, in Wellbeing, Space and Society, Volume 2, 2021

Many of the initial artworks were made using watercolour but, as Autumn gave way to Winter and the seasons progressed, paints were replaced by 'soft' (chalk) pastels. Several of the drawings and paintings were later developed as a series of 'pages', as if found in a notional Book of Hours. Each of Brigid's drawings and paintings of the plants and plant communities was responded to by Christine, poems which necessarily also reflected Christine's personal response to the garden.

We also worked closely with Dr Kitty Wheater, Mindfulness Chaplain at the University of Edinburgh, who went on to compose a series of reflections, as meditations on the effects on body, mind and spirit of time spent this way in the space of this special garden.

In these meditations, Kitty reflects:

> Christine is picking up on something subtle in Brigid's art: the texture gives way … to space and air. It creates a shift in mood that Christine's words echo. The garden is right here, and precious for it, they seem to say – and, too, it reaches out to the great and spacious whole of which it is inextricably part. There is a wonder in this, and the sense of how that seam of love of place gives rise to a love of all place; how the dedication and attention to the micro places love at the heart of the macro…
>
> With dedication and attention come, in turn, both soberness and hope … Love is a practice, we are reminded, and it is a practice embedded in time. It is commitment to the possibility of a future we cannot yet foresee, and mysteries we cannot yet understand, wrapped in that entangled private … world. In commitment, there is surrender to plants, who they are, and all that they unknowably hold.

"It is this that I take away from Brigid and Christine's work: we are different from plants, and this, wonderfully, is the gift of our deep mutuality."

Dr Kitty Wheater, Mindfulness Chaplain, University of Edinburgh

Towards the end of Brigid's time as Artist in Residence in the garden, a short film introducing our collaboration was conceived and filmed by Martin Burt of Native Film. The residency culminated in an exhibition, *Of Mutual Things…*, at Thomson's Tower in the garden, during which a series of talks and a poetry walk were hugely popular events. As time has passed, our collaboration – rather than abruptly ending – has evolved naturally, beyond the perceived confines of a calendar year, onto the pages of this book and back out, into the world.

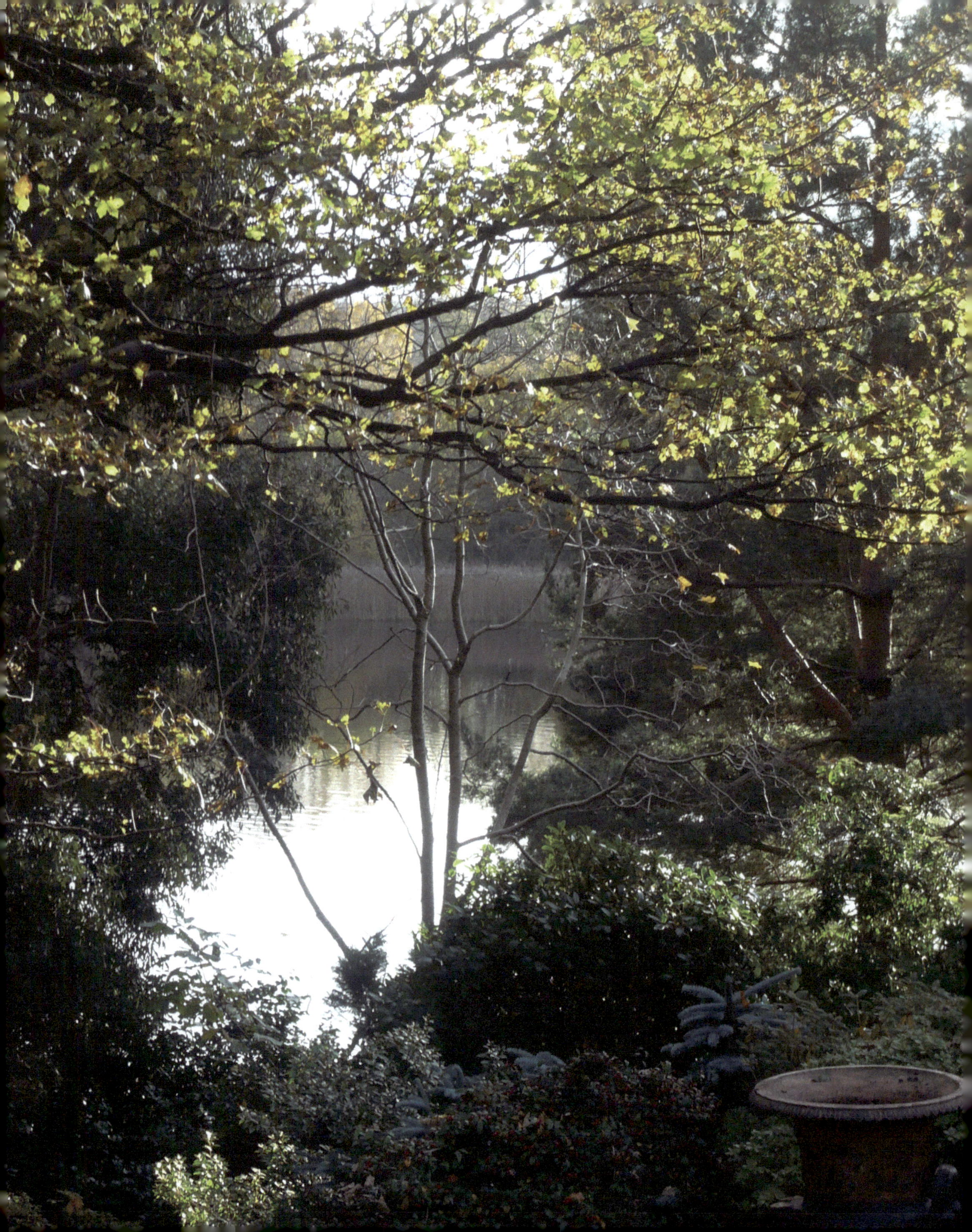

Dr Neil's Garden

Brigid Collins and Christine De Luca

"People experienced a sense of joy, beauty, and reassurance, a greater attunement to the natural world and an increased sense of nature connection than they had at other times: birds felt louder. These heightened sensory and emotional experiences had therapeutic benefits across age and geographical spectrums, during these difficult times."

Wellbeing, Space and Society

Lying as it does along the rugged lower slopes of Arthur's Seat and fringed to the south by Duddingston Loch, Dr Neil's Garden is a secluded haven, sometimes referred to as Edinburgh's Secret Garden. It comprises part of the old grounds attached to the characterful 12th century Duddingston Kirk and benefits, on three sides, from high sandstone walls. The site is indeed dramatic, but this garden is the result of the imagination, dedication and sheer hard work of two local GPs, Drs. Andrew and Nancy Neil who, in the 1960s, created it from a wilderness. It was to become a space in which they encouraged and often 'prescribed' their patients to help with gardening tasks or just to relax and find healing of body, mind and spirit in peaceful and beautiful surroundings.

In one corner of what was to become the garden is Thomson's Tower, a small octagonal building designed in 1825 by William Henry Playfair for the Duddingston Curling Society. The upper floor was used both as meeting place for the curlers and as a studio for the Rev John Thomson, the local minister from 1805 to 1840. He was also a respected artist. The lower floor, adjacent to the loch and used to store the curling stones, is now a tiny museum of curling.

The planting is mostly conifers, heathers and alpines, with primulas (including the rare Pubescens), magnolias, rhododendrons, azaleas and numerous other shrubs. As well as being home to many birds – doves, swans, geese, ducks, waders, owls – frogs, butterflies, and an abundance of insects are found there. Each plant, each tree, each mushroom is home to a myriad of smaller life forms.

In 1997, Dr Neil's Garden Trust was formed, in order to take over the running of the garden, and to safeguard its

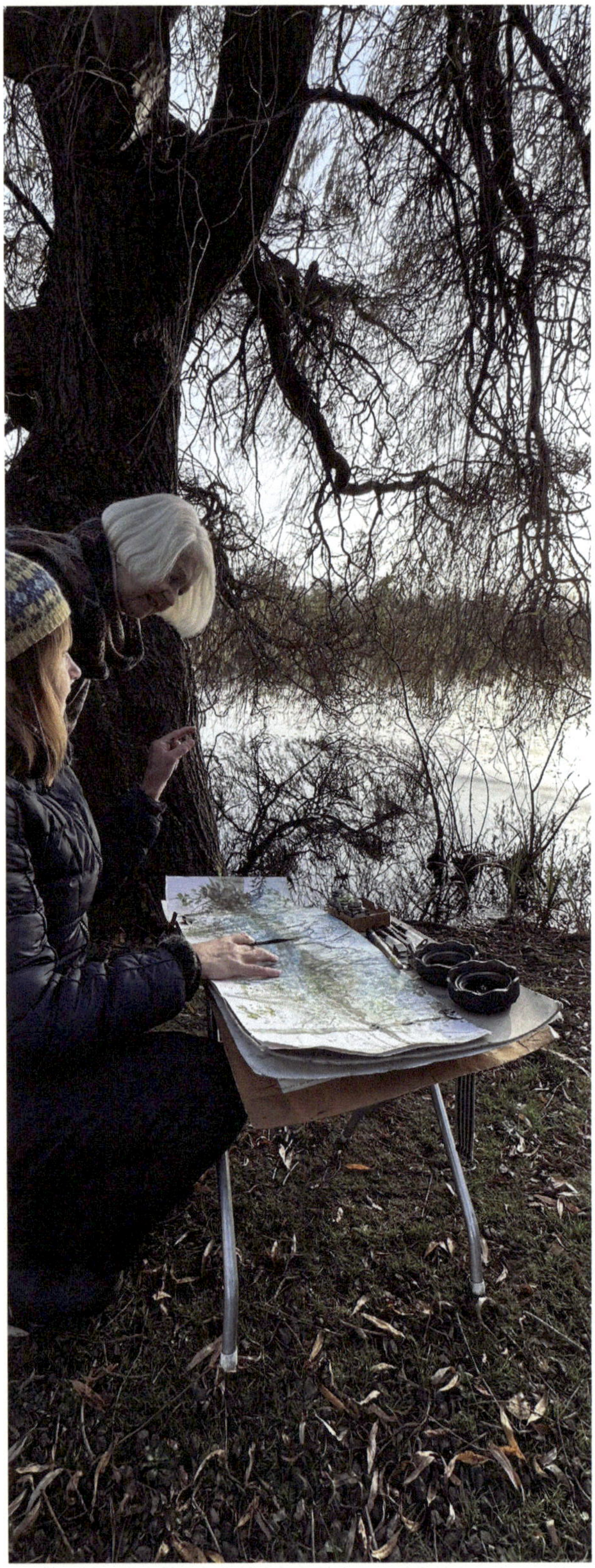

future. The Garden Trust is a registered charity. Following the death of both Andrew and Nancy Neil in 2005, a small Physic Garden was laid out in 2012 and formally opened a year later to commemorate their lives as doctors and gardeners and to highlight their life-long interest in the interconnection between horticulture and wellbeing.

Until recently the garden was tended devotedly and knowledgeably by Claudia Pottier, who, as head gardener, along with a band of dedicated volunteers, cultivated a delicate balance by tending without manicuring. This happily continues to be the *modus operandi* under the keen eyes and hands of the current gardener, Alan Mitchell.

Dr Neil's Garden is so much more than a garden: to many people it has been a place of inspiration – artistic, literary, and spiritual – as well as offering that tranquillity necessary for contemplation. It is a friendly place that welcomes all to its peace and beauty and, at the same time, offers comradeship and training to volunteers from many walks of life. It is a place in which change is stimulated through play, learning, the arts, physical activity, and by addressing the special needs of many people; where nature merges with culture, where cultivation and civilisation are nurtured. It is a place that encourages a looking outwards, as well as a looking inwards, a place where, by spending time, we realise the futility of putting ourselves at the centre of the universe; where a 'putting back together' of things and of ourselves becomes a possibility that is rooted in reality.

time reshapes the works of love:
a conversation of petals tuned
to the season's rallentando.
our wrap of memory sustains
such fragile futures.

– Christine De Luca

SPRING

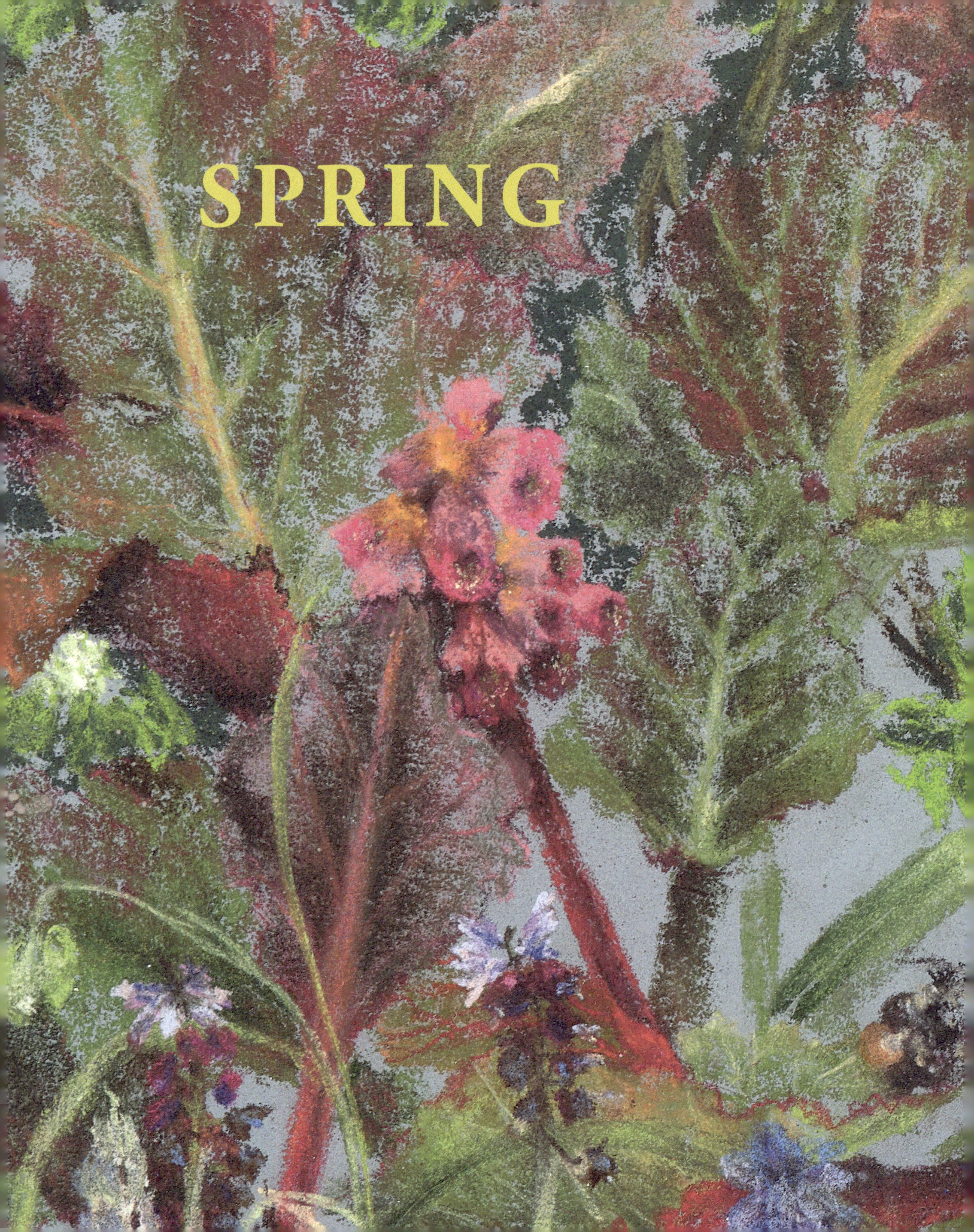

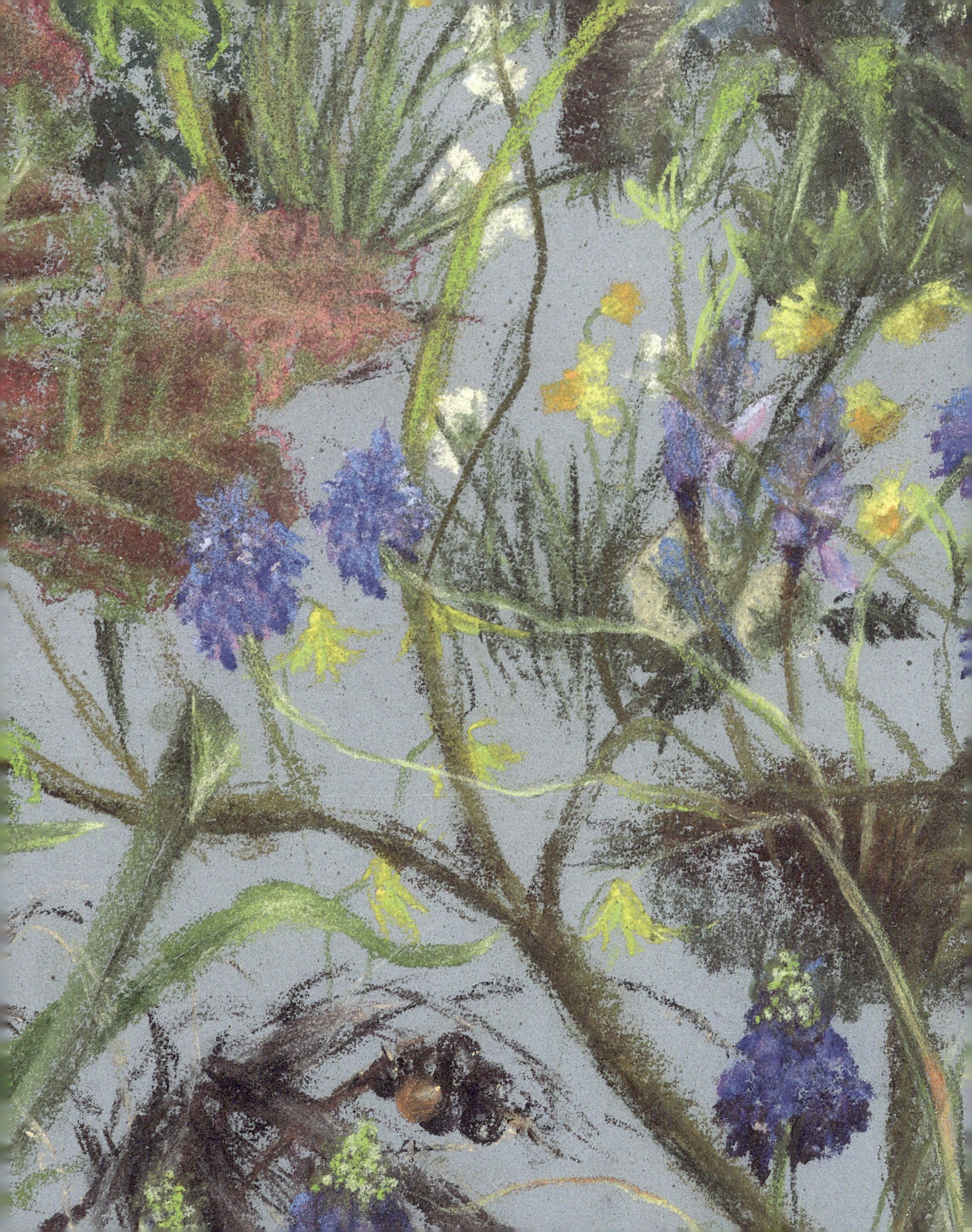

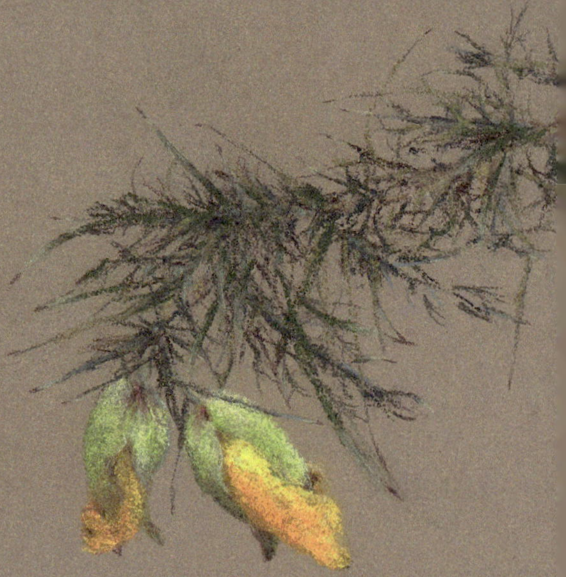

The pleasing shock of the exotic

Magnolia against Crow Hill

You waken to our Scottish Spring, bringing,
as if from another world, the pleasing shock
of the exotic. All that inner life, that innate energy:

furred buds that peel back revealing waxy goblets;
a panoply, an oriental lusciousness that teases
the arms of that old elm, chides its slow progress to

tasselled glory. As you open and the sun picks you out,
you brighten haunts, flourish and flaunt.
Do you dim to candle light in the dark?

These grasses too have come a distance, fitted in,
acclimatised to our ways. They enliven the garden,
soften the line of Crow Hill that will only offer gorse.

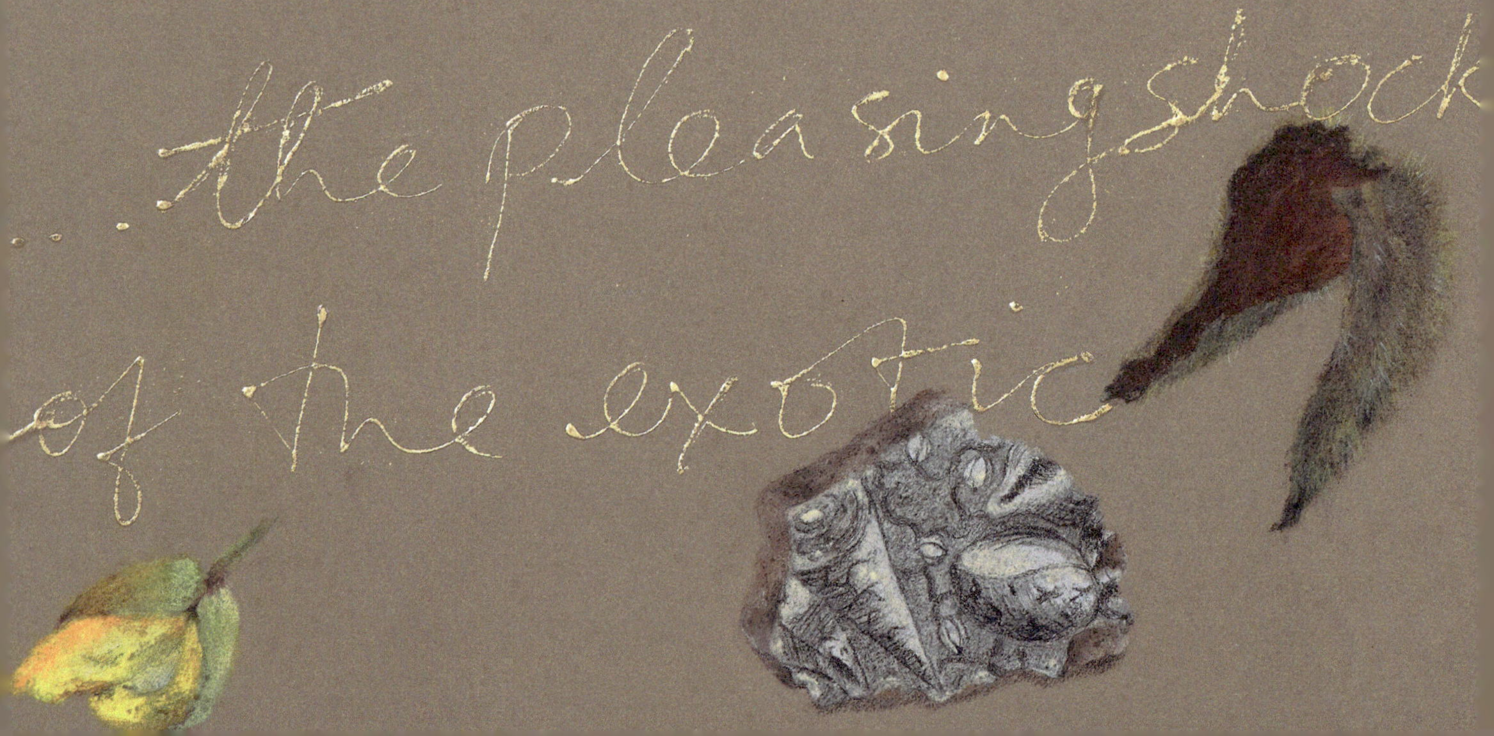

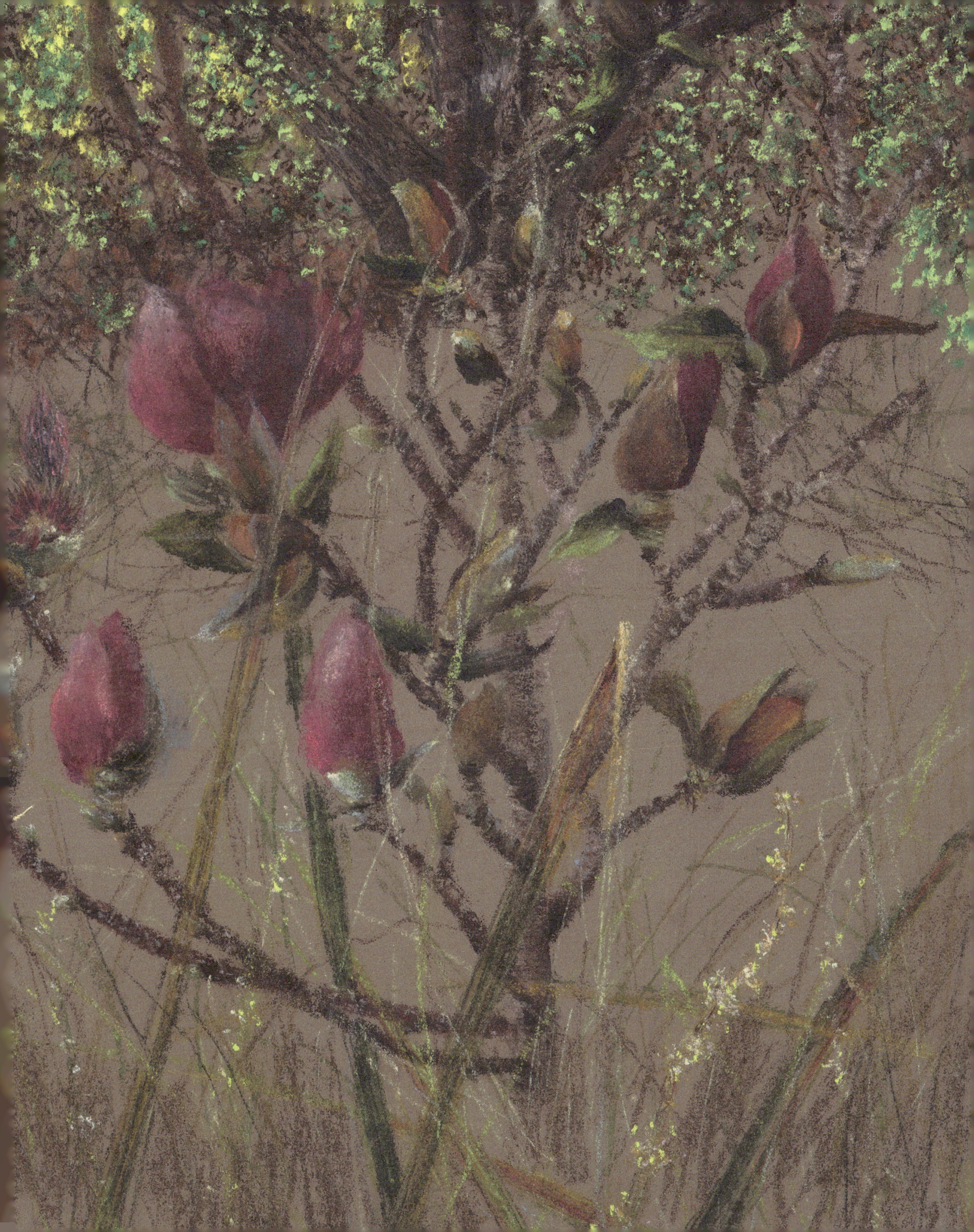

Robin's pincushion

Moss Gall

Past

When shrivelled up in summer
moss galls were squirrelled under pillows
to summon sleep, hung round necks
to ease rheumatics, tucked
in coat-cuffs to avoid a flogging.

Present

A wily wasp can trick a thicket rose
to grow that gall to house its offspring:
a shady larder to see them through the seasons,
from eggs to larvae – a prickly pompom
pulsing with pupae, their swinging cradle.

That bright-eyed robin: is he biding his time,
counting the months; hoar frost on fir, perfume
of viburnum, May buds on the old rose till,
at last, he will dart as wasps emerge, unfold
wings, depart, take flight across the loch?

Future

It's a struggle to like the wasp, despite
all that pollinating, useful foraging.
But who knows what gifts, what remedies
might languish in such oddball chemistry;
in such harmonious entanglements?

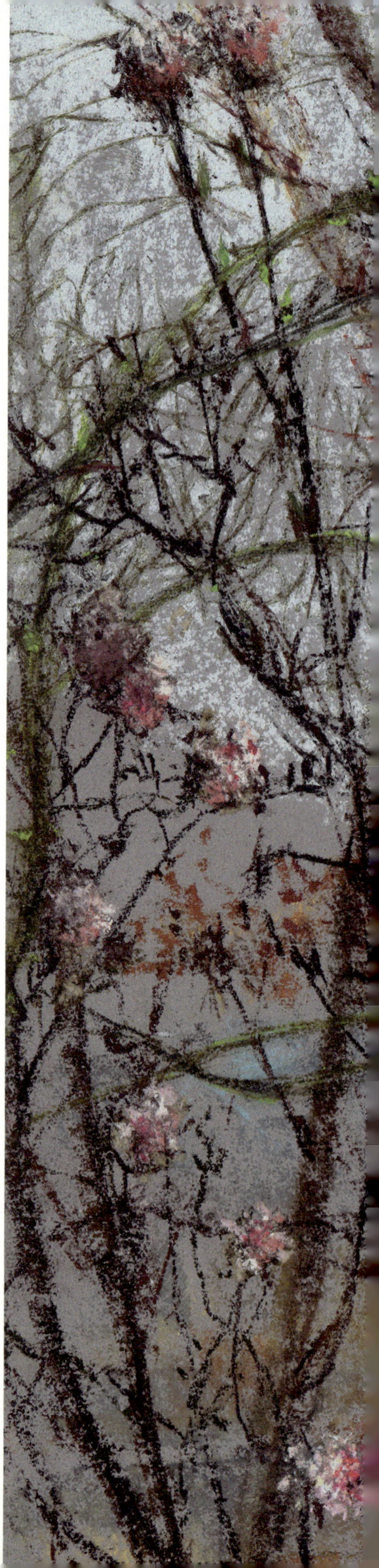

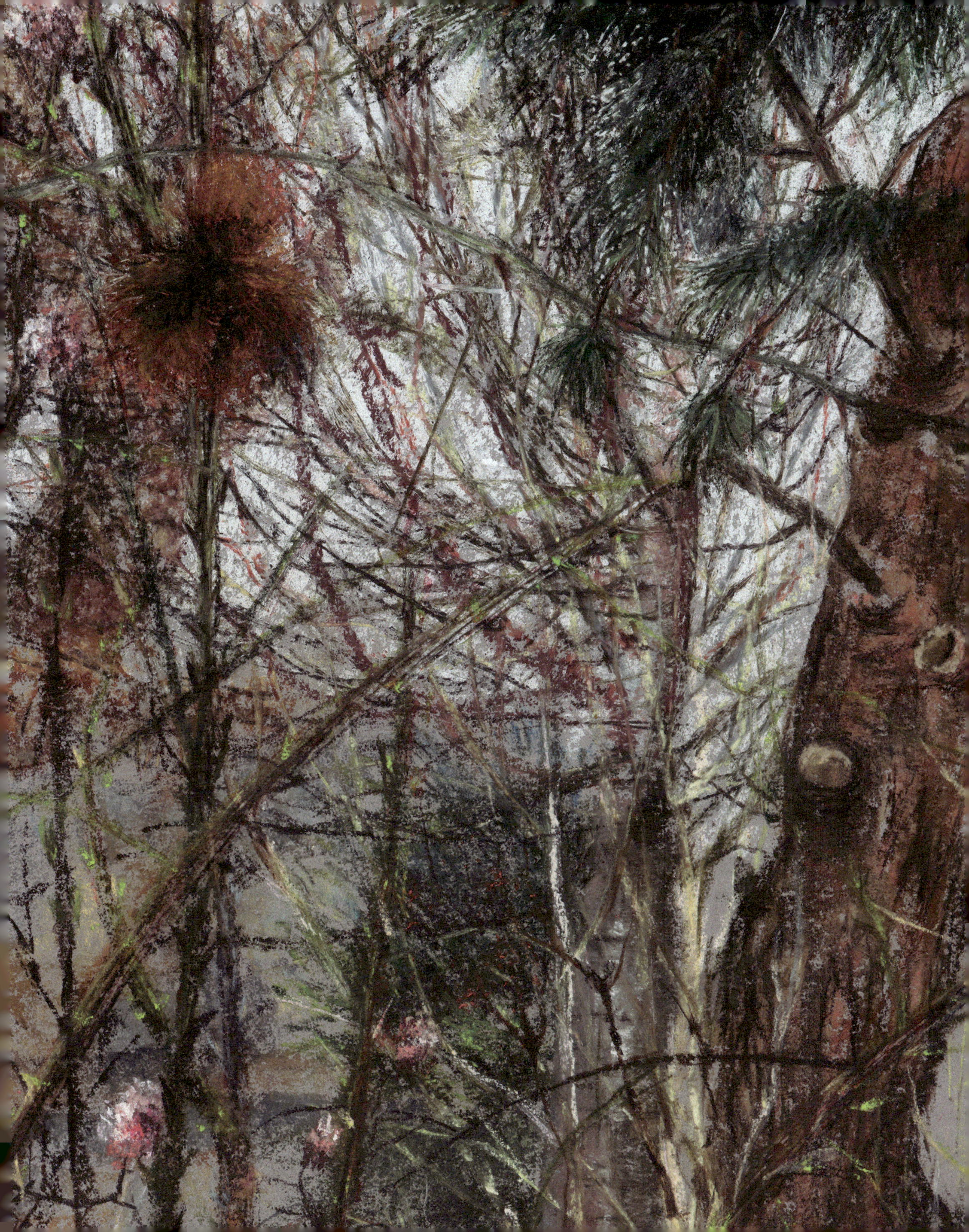

A kind of mirth

Apricot, acer and friends

Unseasonal buds of apricot are bursting,
bright pink with lemon stamens.
They sprinkle naked branches
with a kind of mirth, a smile
behind the hands; a delicate intensity.
A bumblebee could get drunk
basting itself in pollen
if it stumbled on the invitation.

Above ground, mutual adorning;
and underground, no doubt,
a secret sociability and care.
The acer, still bare, will stun us
later, with subtle shades turning
from brightest green to red; while
blousy euphorbia will push itself
forward, exploiting a gap.

Meanwhile the hill and the kirk
are bit parts; the wind off the loch
murmurs the firs and a piper
accompanies all the little birds.

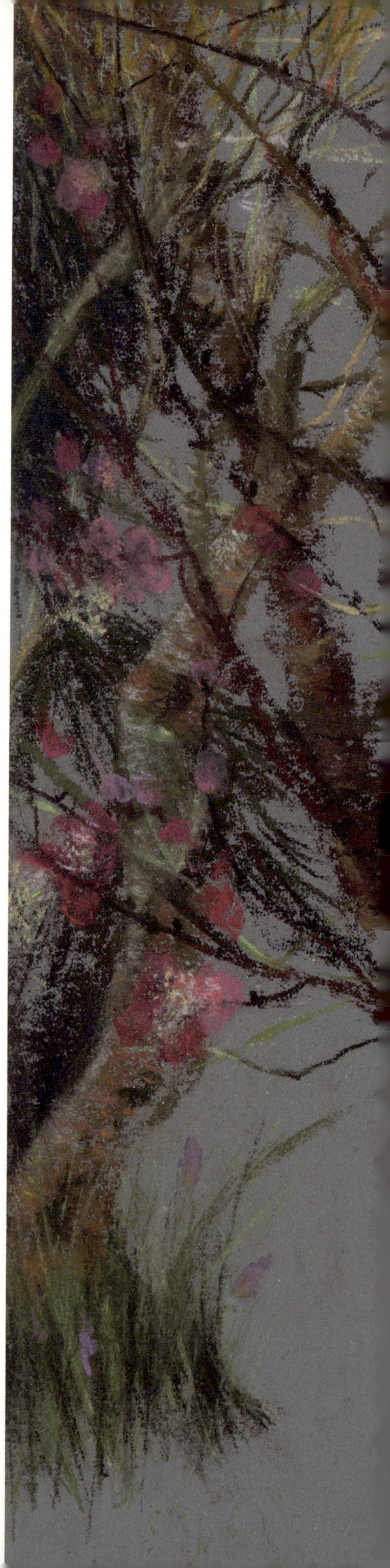

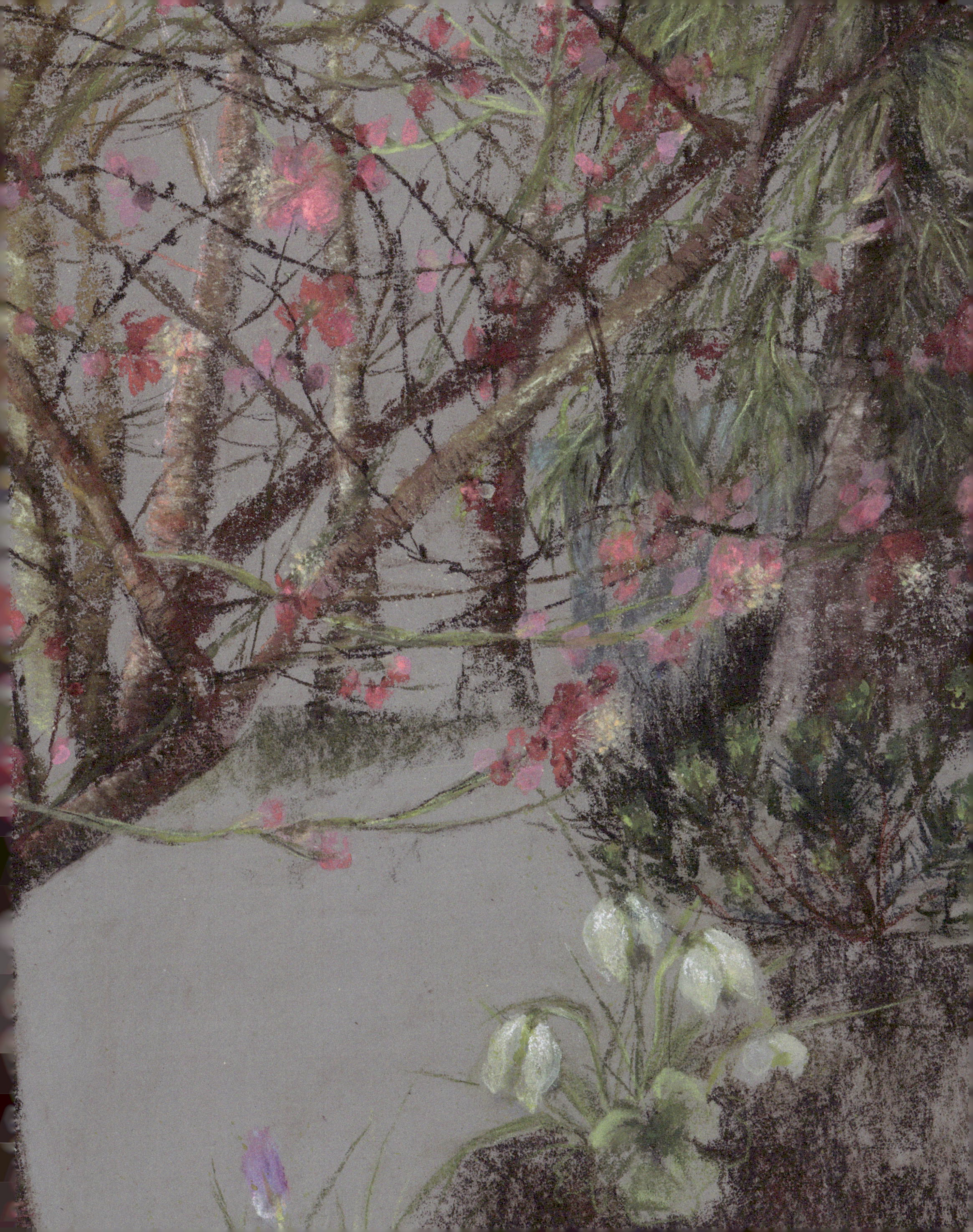

Under the Willow

It is unmistakeably Spring, though
the birches are barely budding
and the hawthorn still counting
the days till may-time. It's the willow
that's up and running; its cape draped
in fronds that sway, touch the water.
Low light plays off the loch
till all is luminescing.

Geese are pairing up: a little timely
neck-dipping will seal their bond.
They are inquisitive about each other;
curious too about their reedy bed, fringed
with fleshy flowers. Near the Tower, where
couples loiter, their nuptial canopy is
those airy birches, tickle of willow
and the long memory of hawthorn.

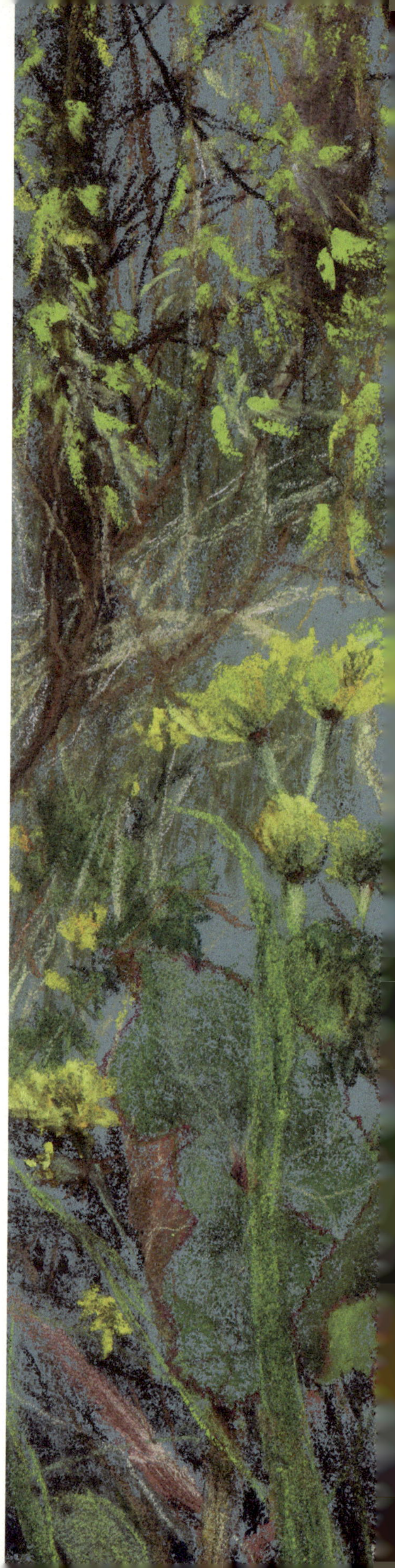

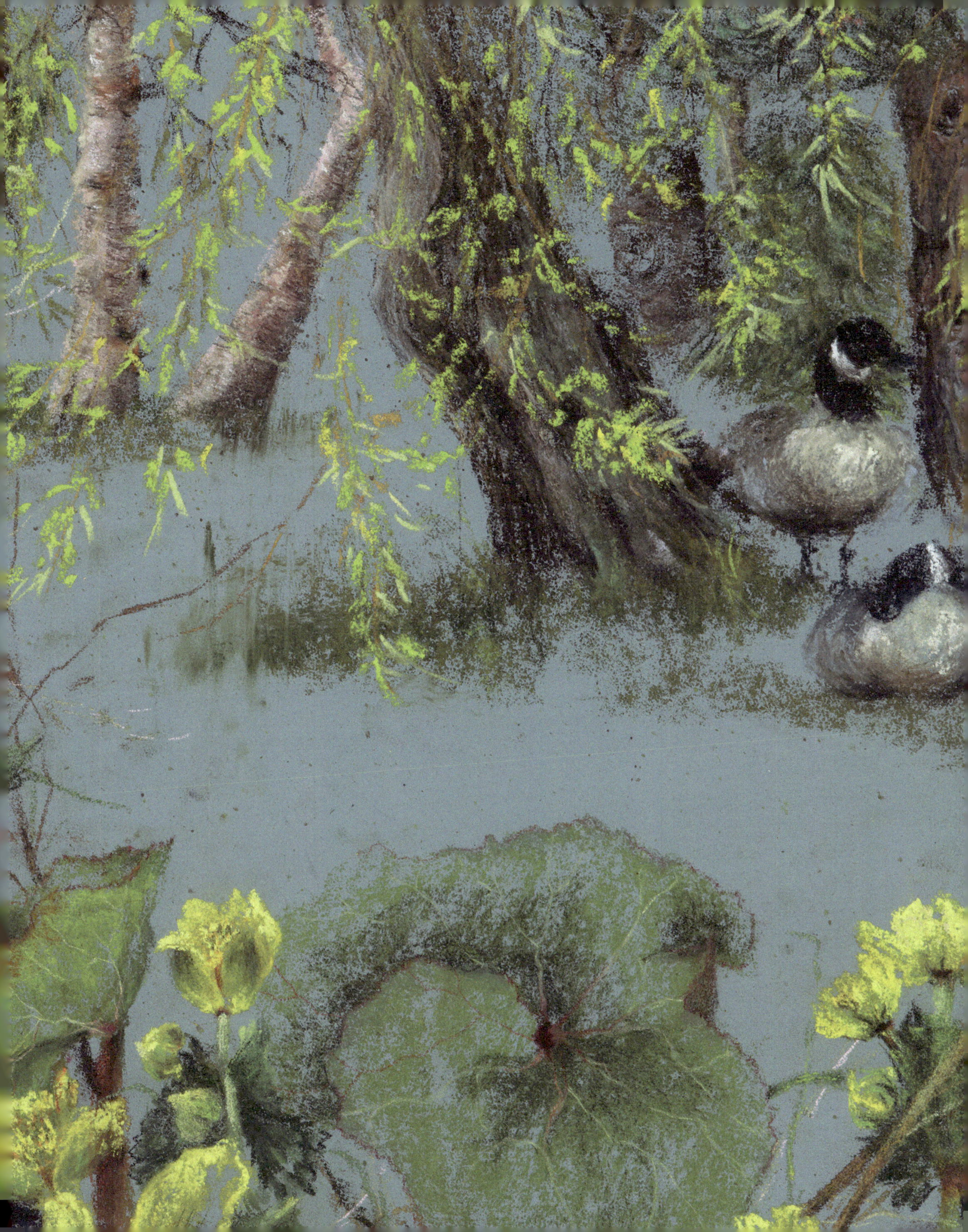

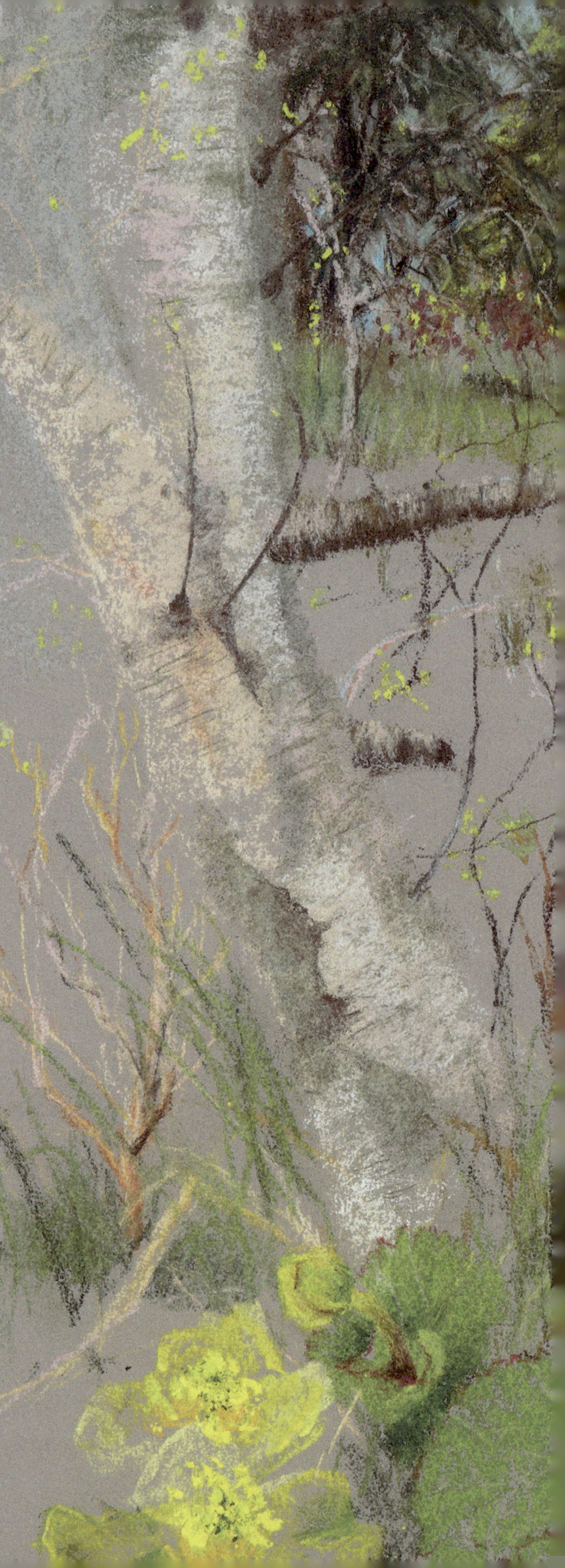

Silver and gold

Against a backdrop of gnarled fir
there's a ballet chancing in the glade:
birches, lithe-bodied, with bark
silk-slipped in silver, and tiniest tears
snagging and scattering light.
New leaves, slivers of gold-leaf,
choreograph joy as they flitter.

The romance goes on, costume-changing
through the seasons, chiding the loch
when it dons a dark dress;
inspiriting all who look closely,
inviting us to dance.

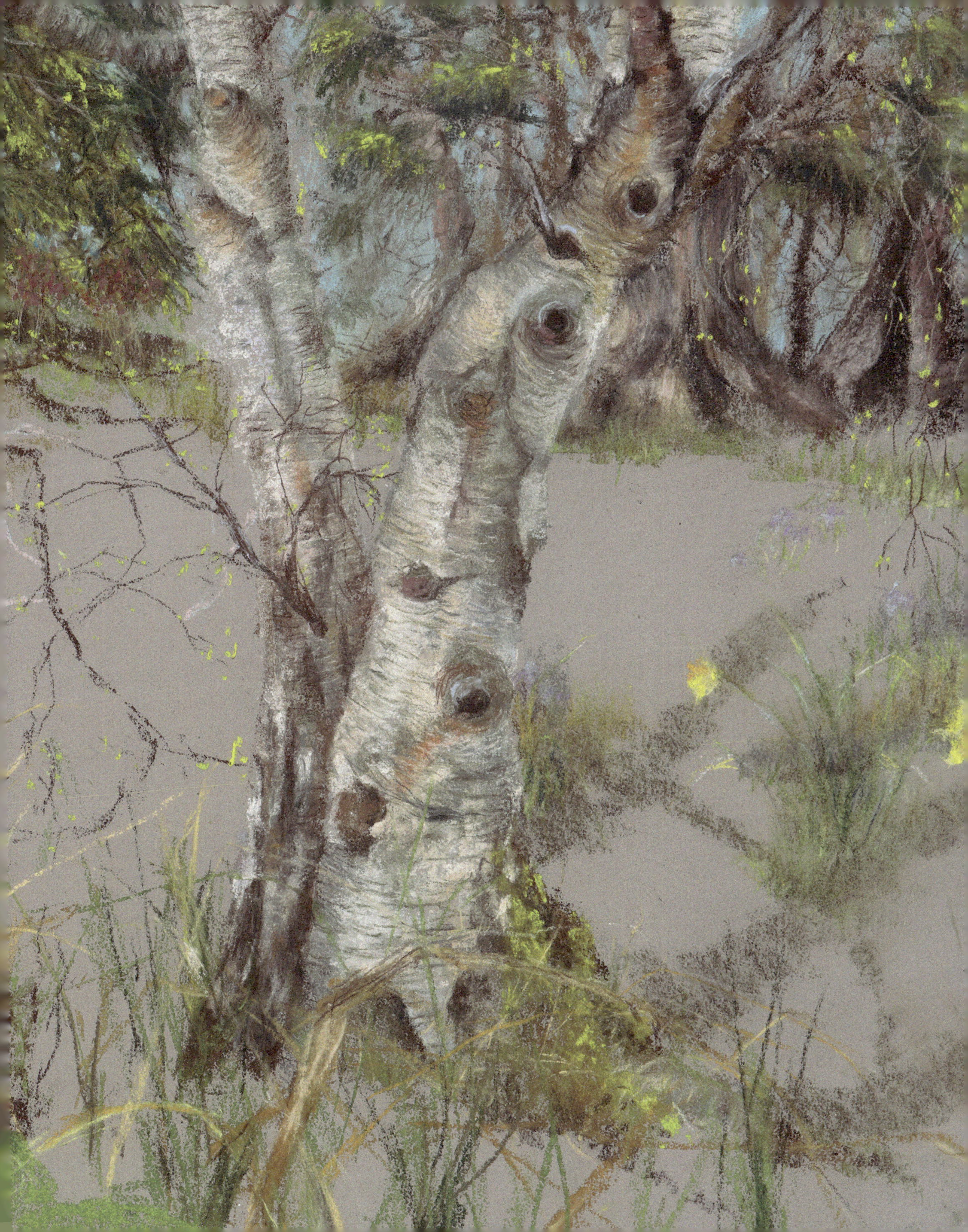

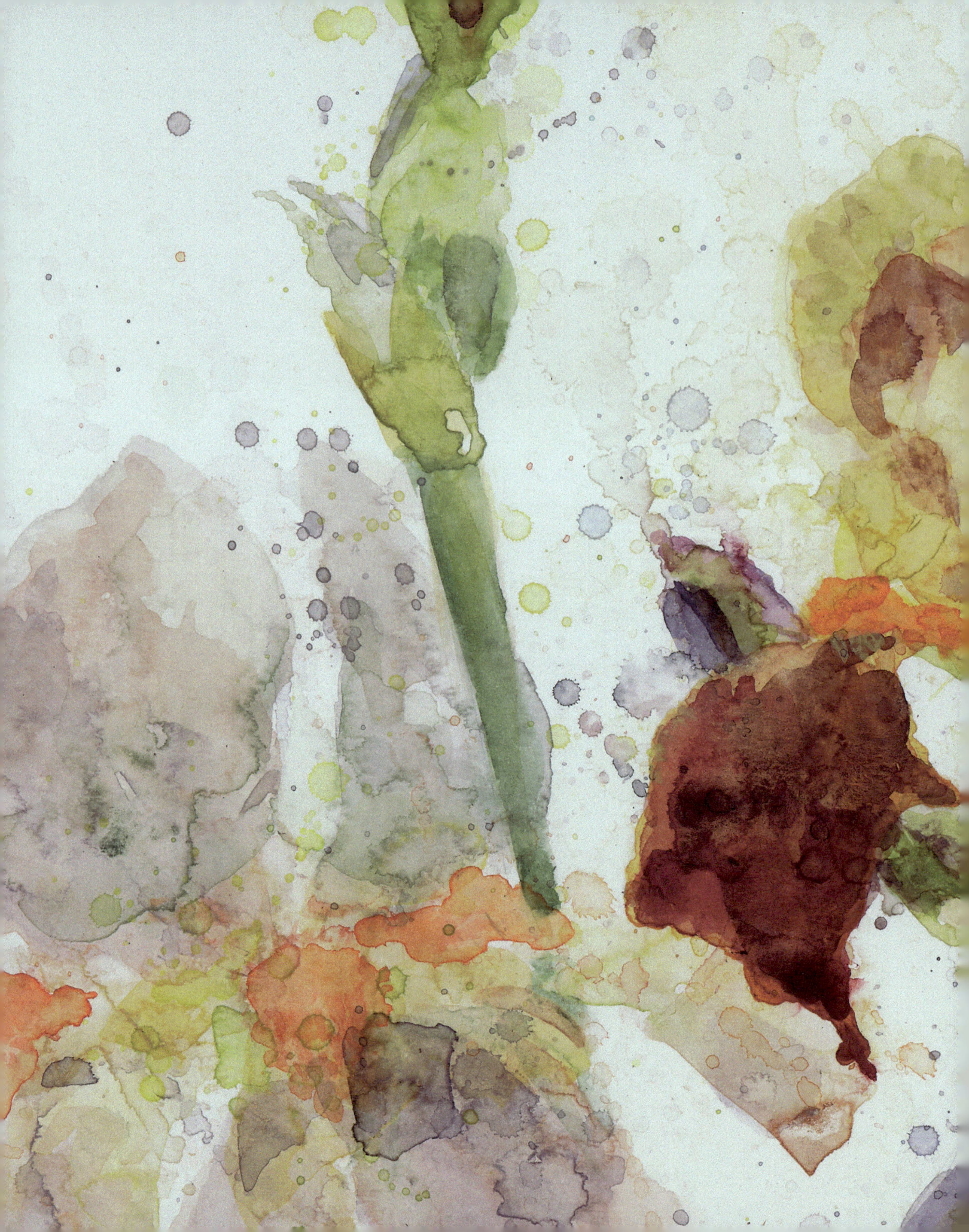

SUMMER

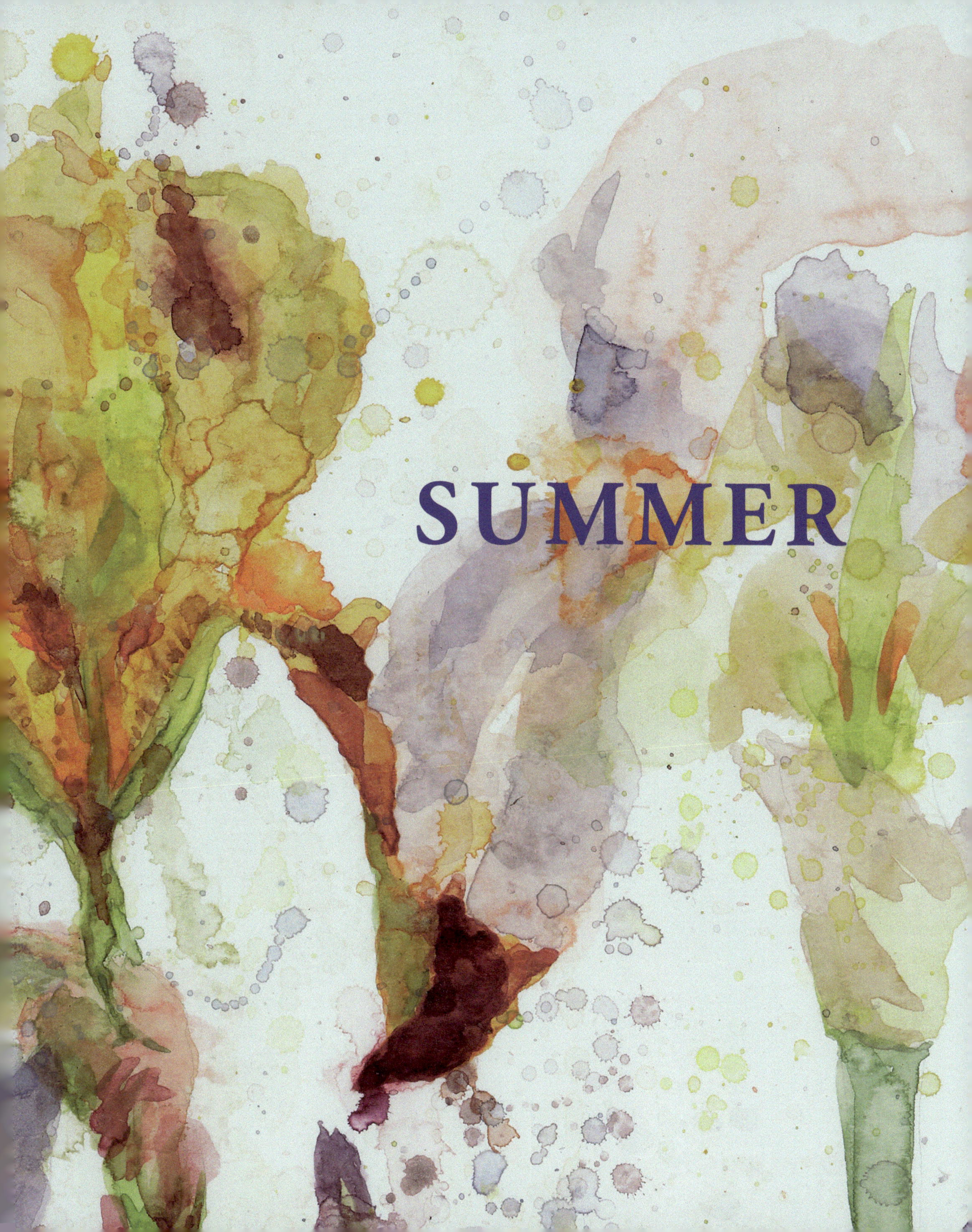

Undimmed

A last iris, late in the season,
still holding every hue:
through all the blues and greens,
tinctures of mauves and violets

colours from Caspian,
tints of the old Silk Road,
tongue to tip
a fine-veined tracery.

Its tissued withering is
a gathering into itself;
a reprise of its first unfolding
and just as lovely.

Time reshapes the works of love:
a conversation of petals tuned
to the season's rallentando.
Our wrap of memory sustains
such fragile futures.

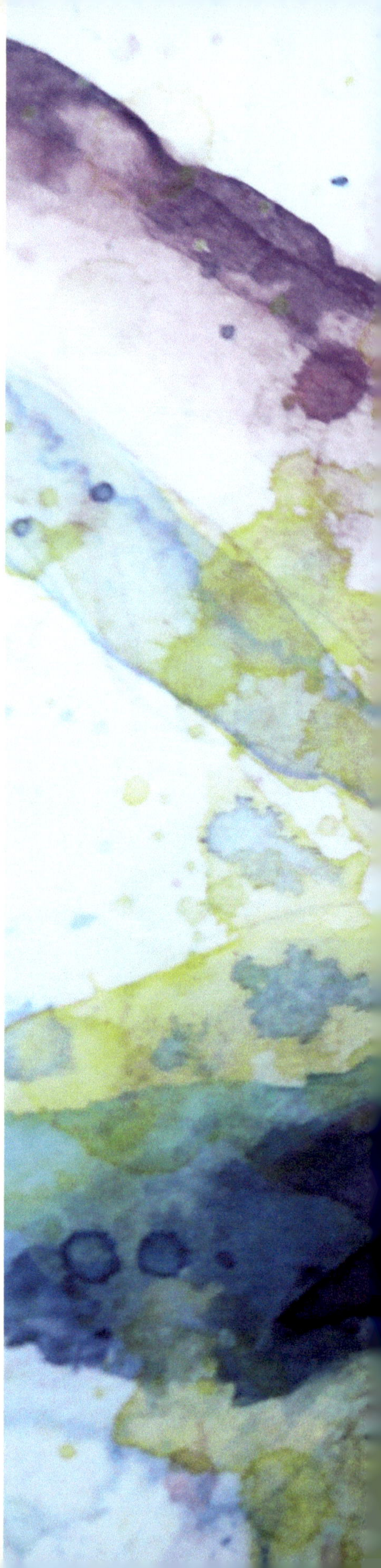

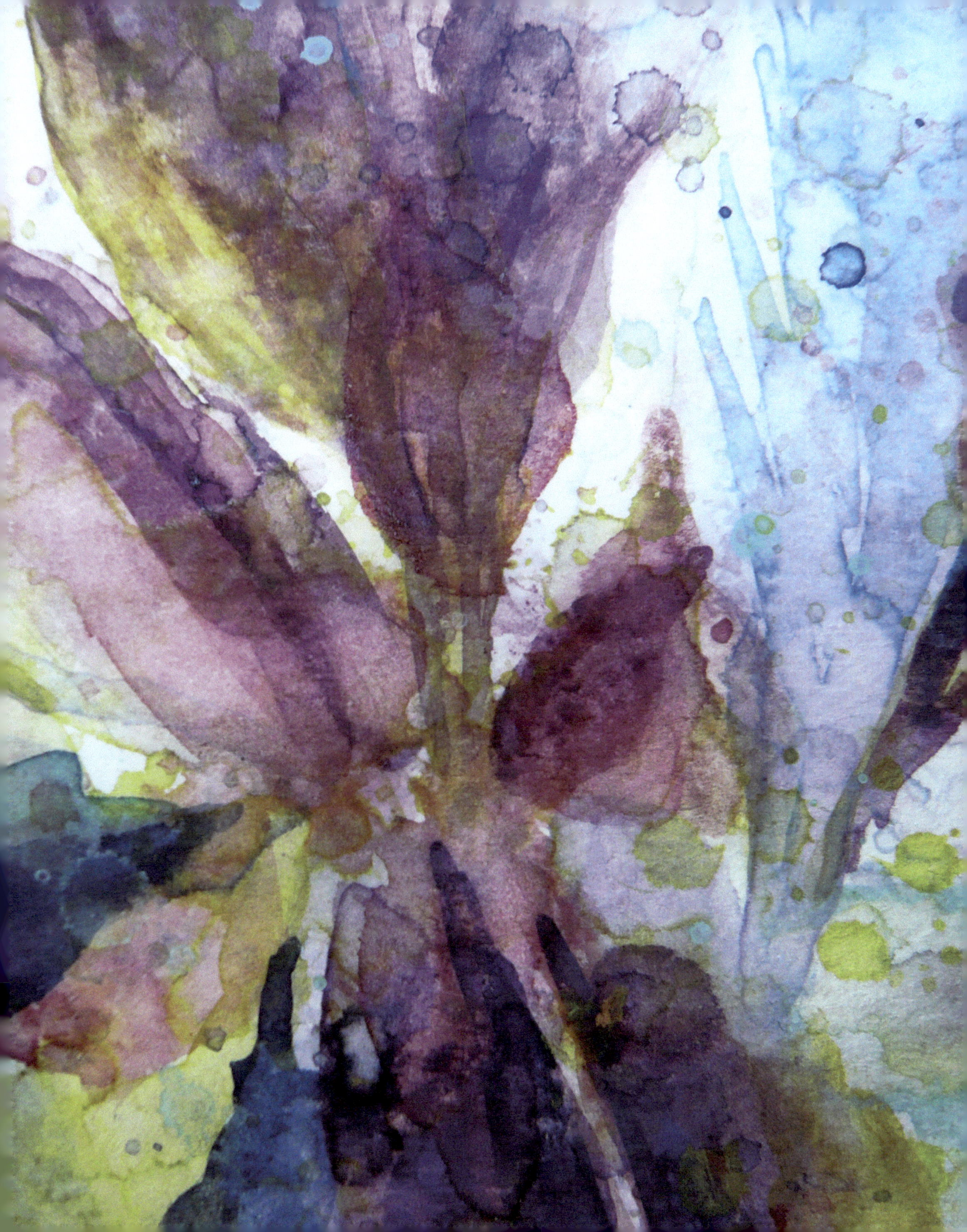

Quantum sufficit

A sufficient quantity

The atoms of the wild rose petals
dance before the eye, create
a heart-shape in the mind, and with
the merging of two such probabilities
(where is the eye? where is the rose?)
decide they like the certainty
the rose brings to the blind.

Sufficient in size is the tiny wild rose
sufficient in staying power: a day
a transience. And the perfume
whose secret atoms break all bounds
all probabilities, conjures a presence.

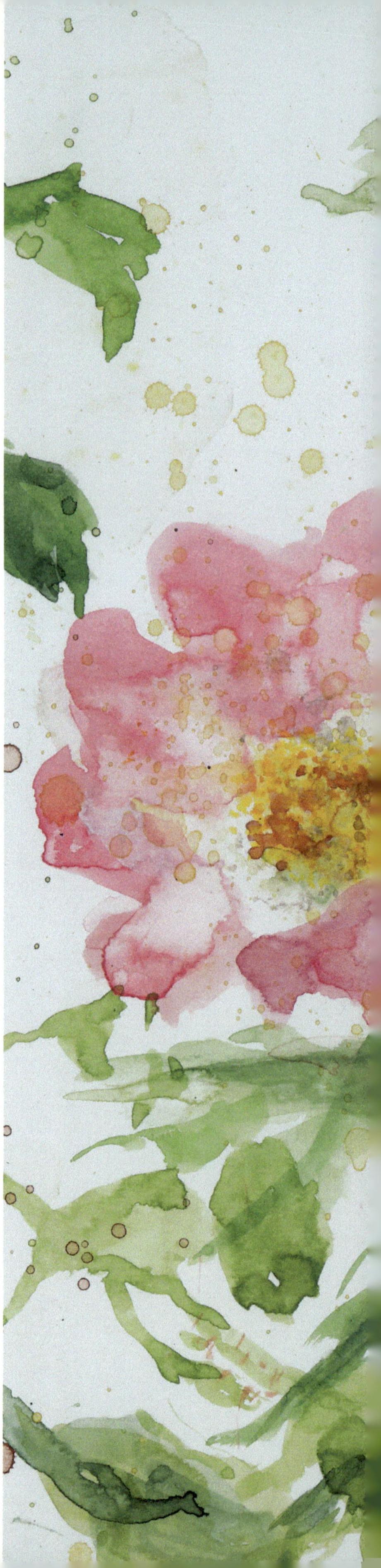

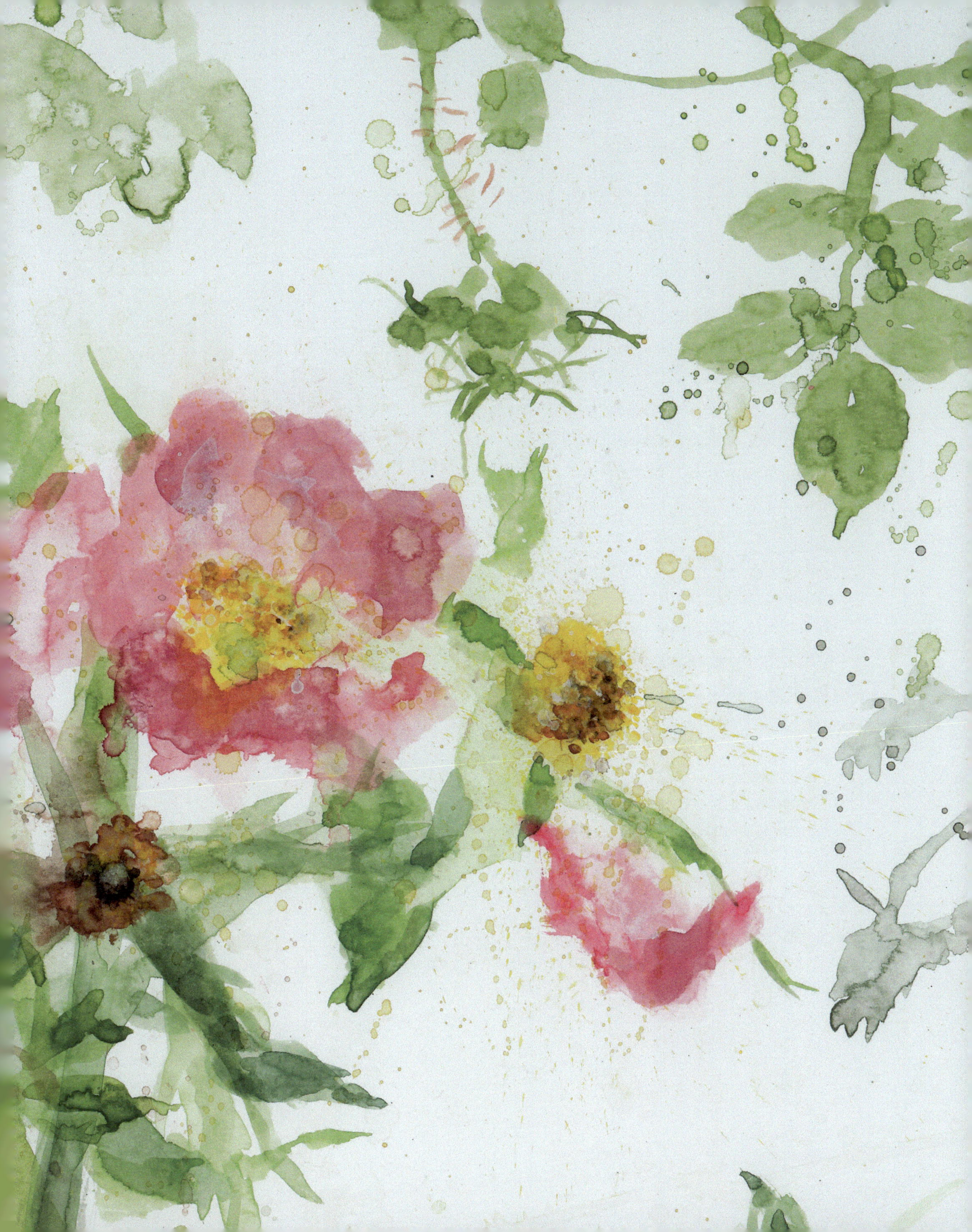

Lull

Dierama pulcherrimum

There's something of the *corps de ballet* about
these grasses. Is it the way they drape,
hold themselves with a lithe grace,
trip in, stage-left, wave on floaty wave,
arrayed in dresses, petunia and cerise
fading, crêpe-thin, to fuchsia?

But that's fanciful: it's just
a breeze off the loch that sets
the slender stem aswing:
a mobile over a ferny cradle,
rocking gently. '*Hark,*
what peaceful music rings.'

(from 'Jesu, joy of man's desiring', by J S Bach,
translated by Robert Bridges)

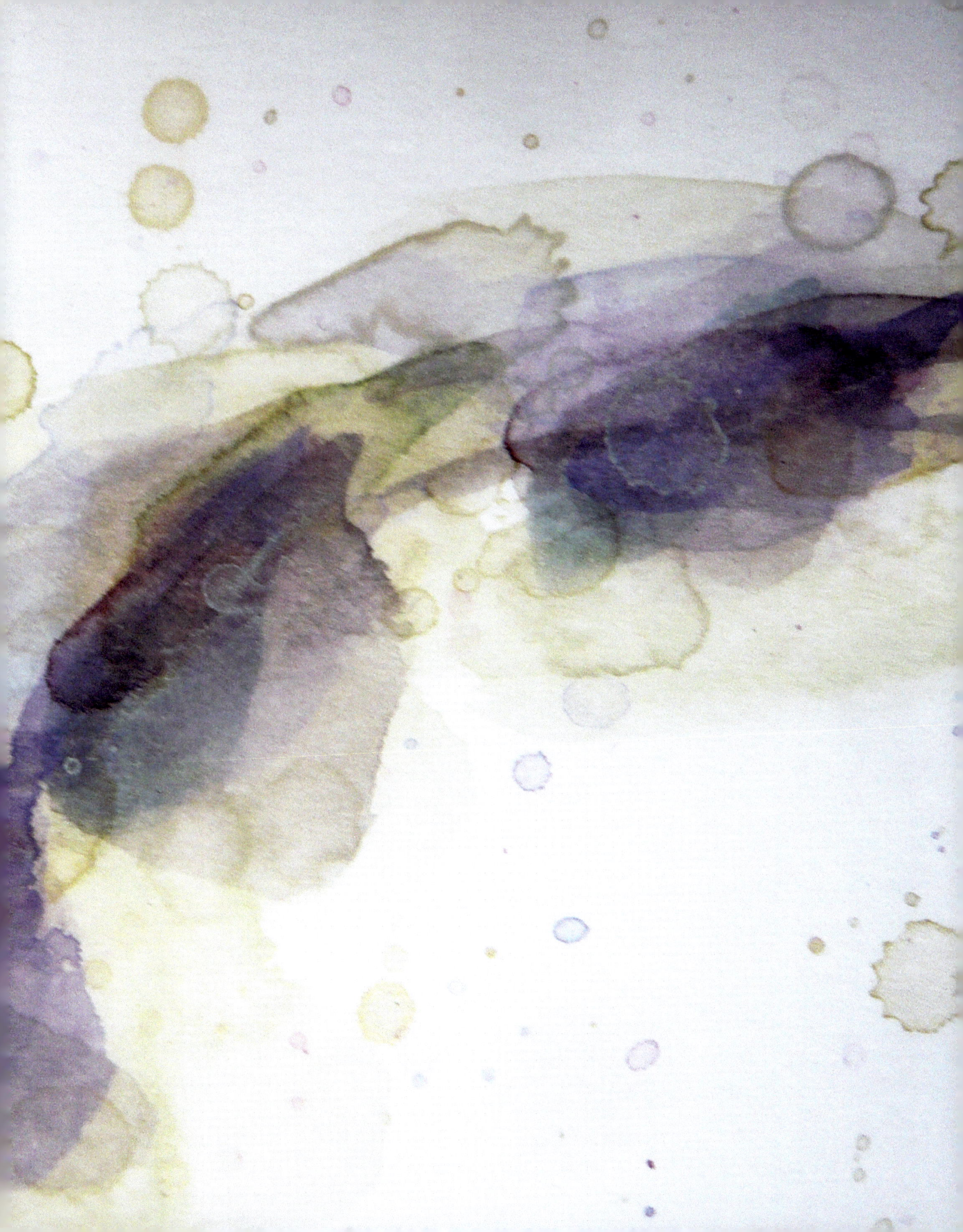

Drowning in wonder

Clover

Even if
your pink heads weren't so perfect
or you had no perfume
or little nectar

Even if
you had two leaves
or four
rather than a perfect three

You would still be valuable
for hay-making
for soil nutrients
for suppressing weeds
for breaking hard-pan clay
for drainage

If I were a bumblebee
I'd drown in your wonder
pollinate acres

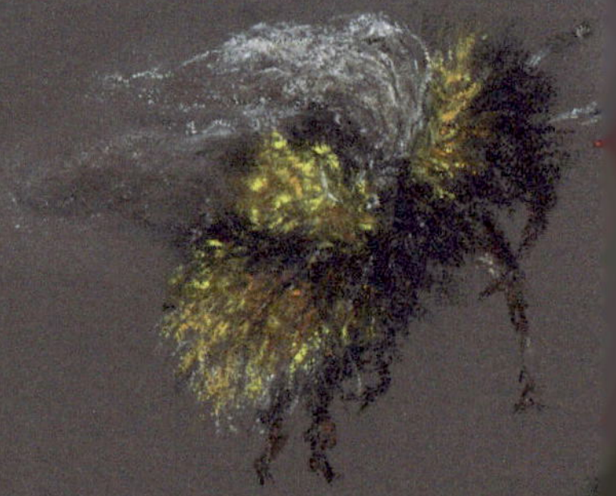

I'd drown in your wor

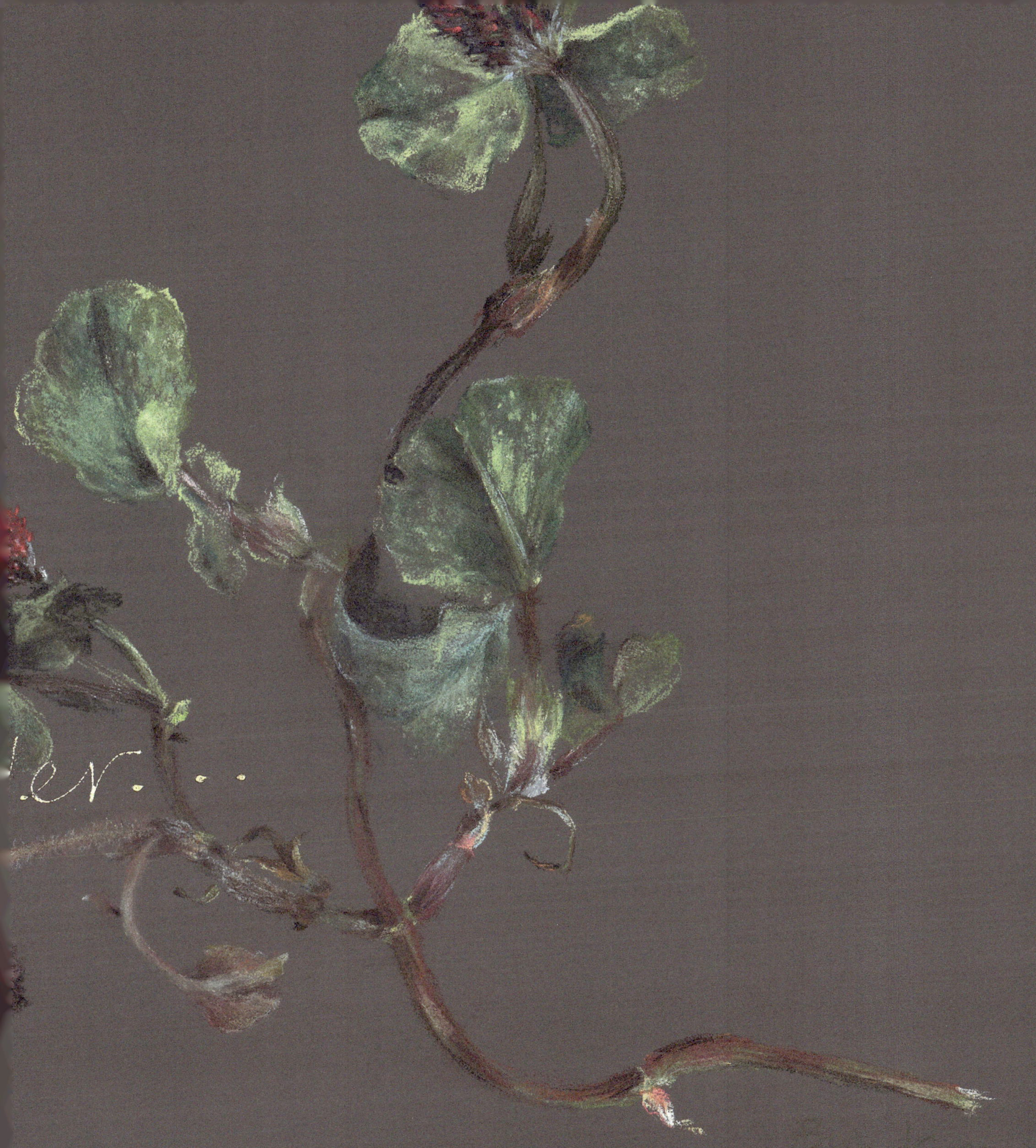

When the world feels broken

Though the rowan has veered offstage, it's left us
its crown of blossom: fronds of white,
leaves that filter light over the little pond.
Who will dominate this chronicle? The pines are
merely a backdrop. Perhaps it is the pool itself,
succouring others, bonding them together?

Or darmera, with its pink flowers, stems like rhubarb:
lush-leaved, profuse, longing for mountain streams,
opening its green umbrellas, hoping for showers. It rivals
the brash marsh marigold, Dürer's tufts of cowslip.

All is on cue: grasses and ferns edge in on the mirth.
Once bluebells have faded, there will be water lilies;
and irises will once again stun us to attention,
remind us of the shocking boundlessness of grace.

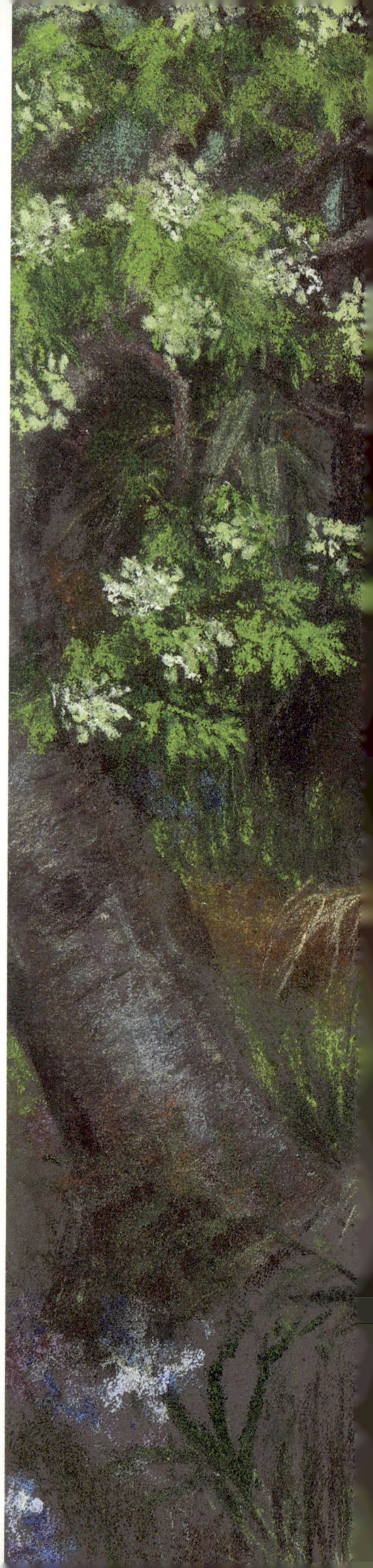

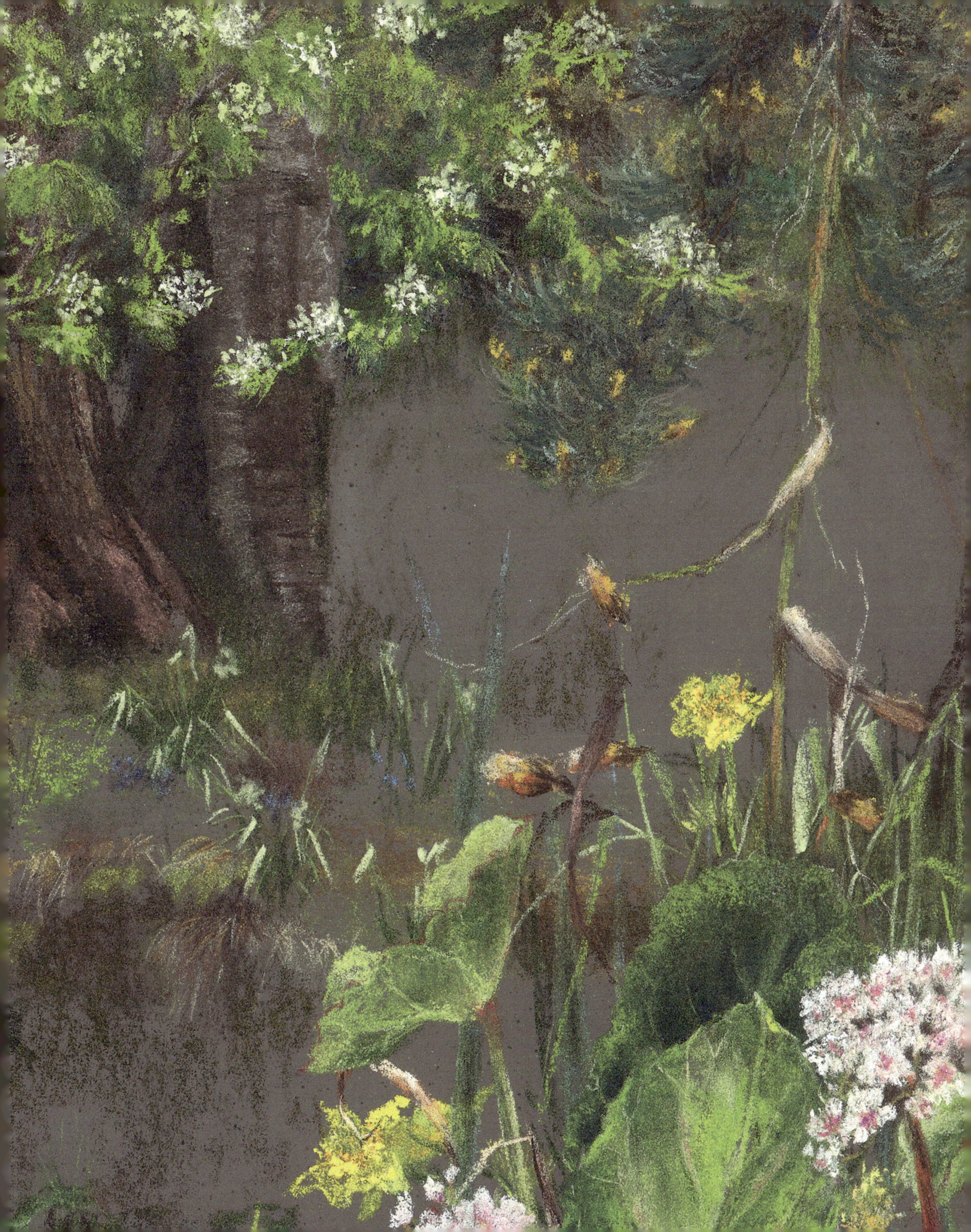

AUTUMN

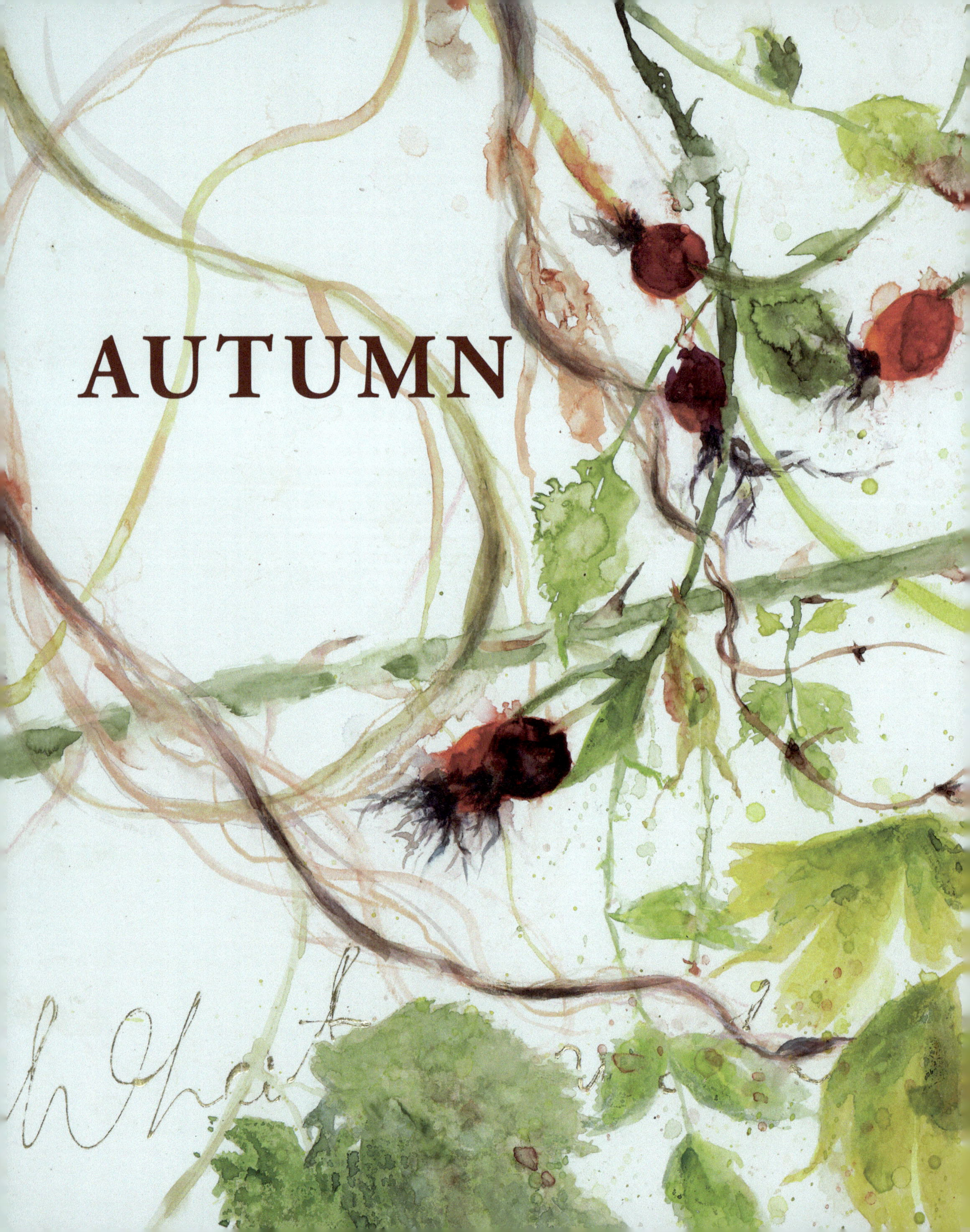

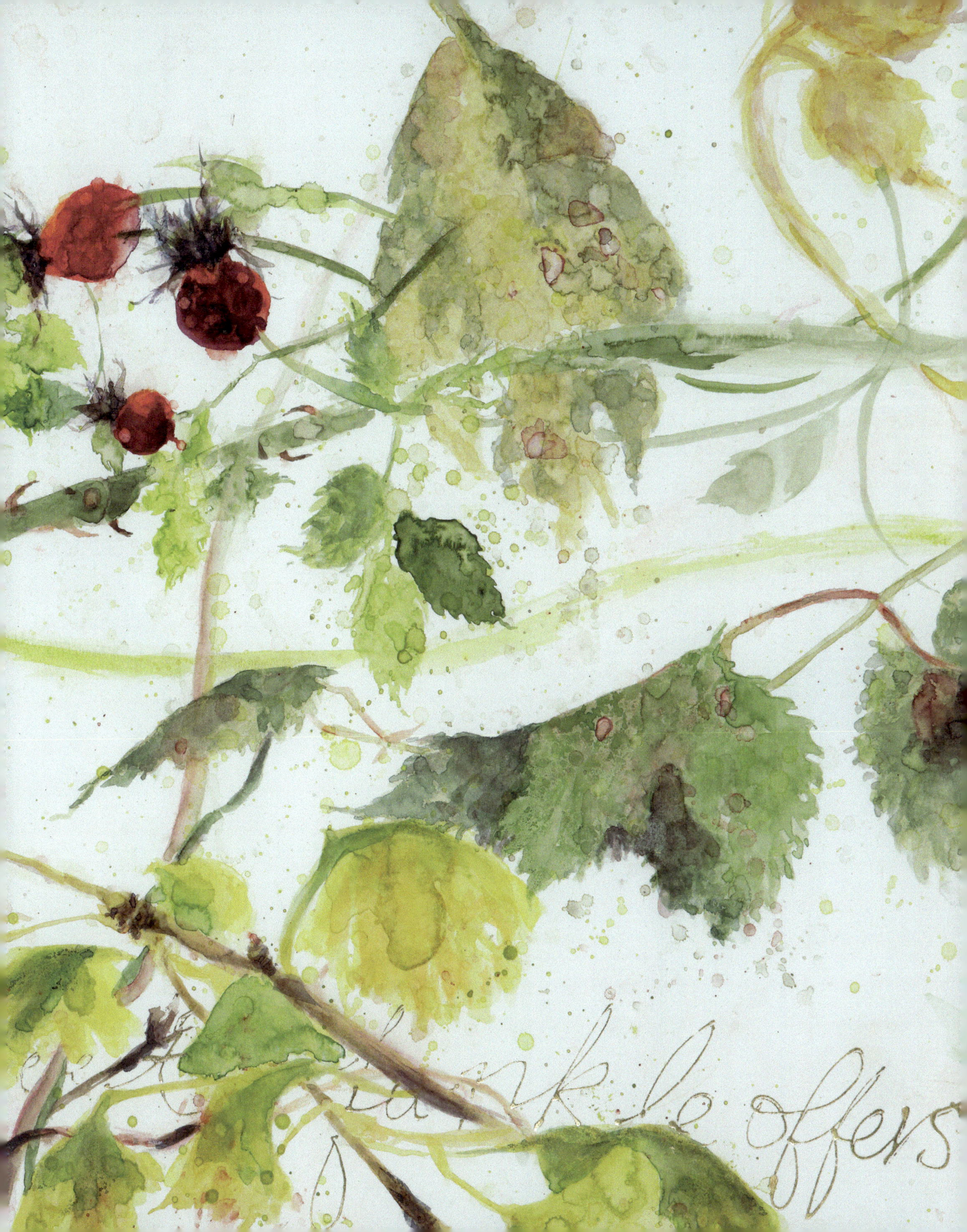
offers

Conversation

It is late in the season, and the conversation
between hop and ginkgo and wild rose is
of mutual things: chatter of shade, support, stability;
of insects, nutrients, water. Braided through
leaves and stems, messages touch deeply, rouse
fungal chums. What such sweet fankle offers.

They are charmed that the artist has picked
them out, detected their communion.
She is part of them now, her face pixelated
in green, her ankles festooned in their tousle.
They paint themselves on her white paper,
make their marks in the long light of afternoon.

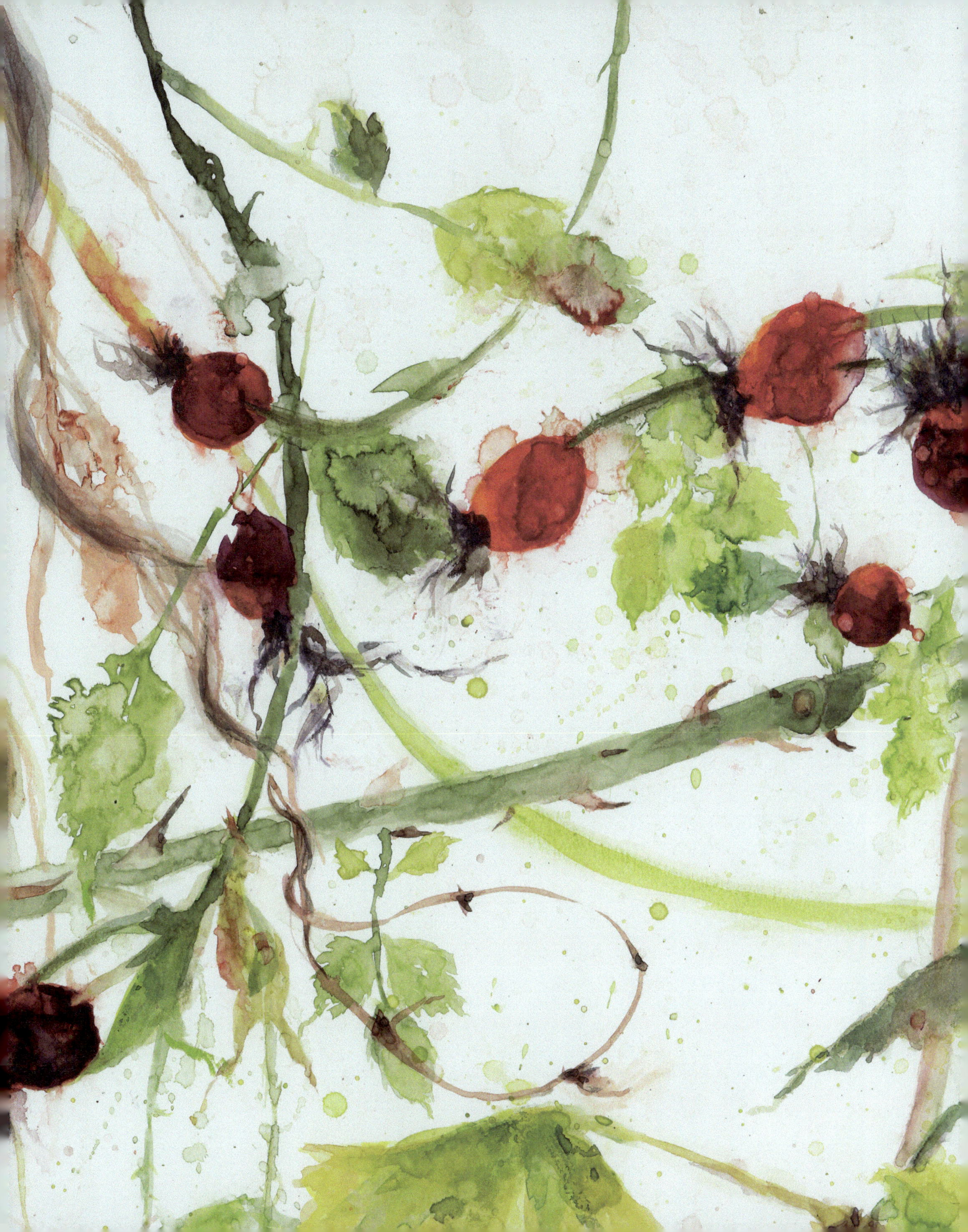

Ginkgo biloba

銀果 *Silver fruit*

Graceful leaves belie
your ancient genome
your resilience.

Slithers of light,
they spring upwards
from the branch,

flick their fans,
curtsey low, perfect
the slowest dance;

or hang downwards,
lime-green butterflies,
a flutter of peace.

You slow
our step
our heartbeat.

Your leaves
shape solace,
seek out communion.

'*The antiquity of a tree is a concentration of cosmic energy*'

—Stanley Kunitz

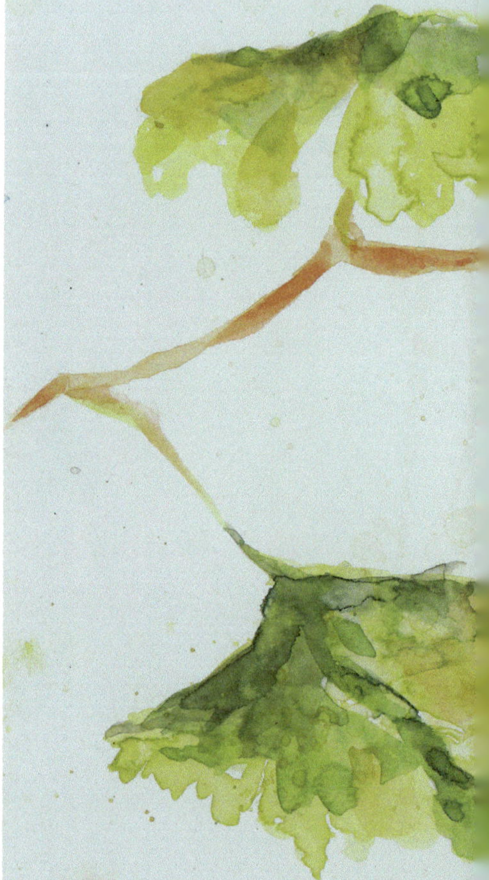

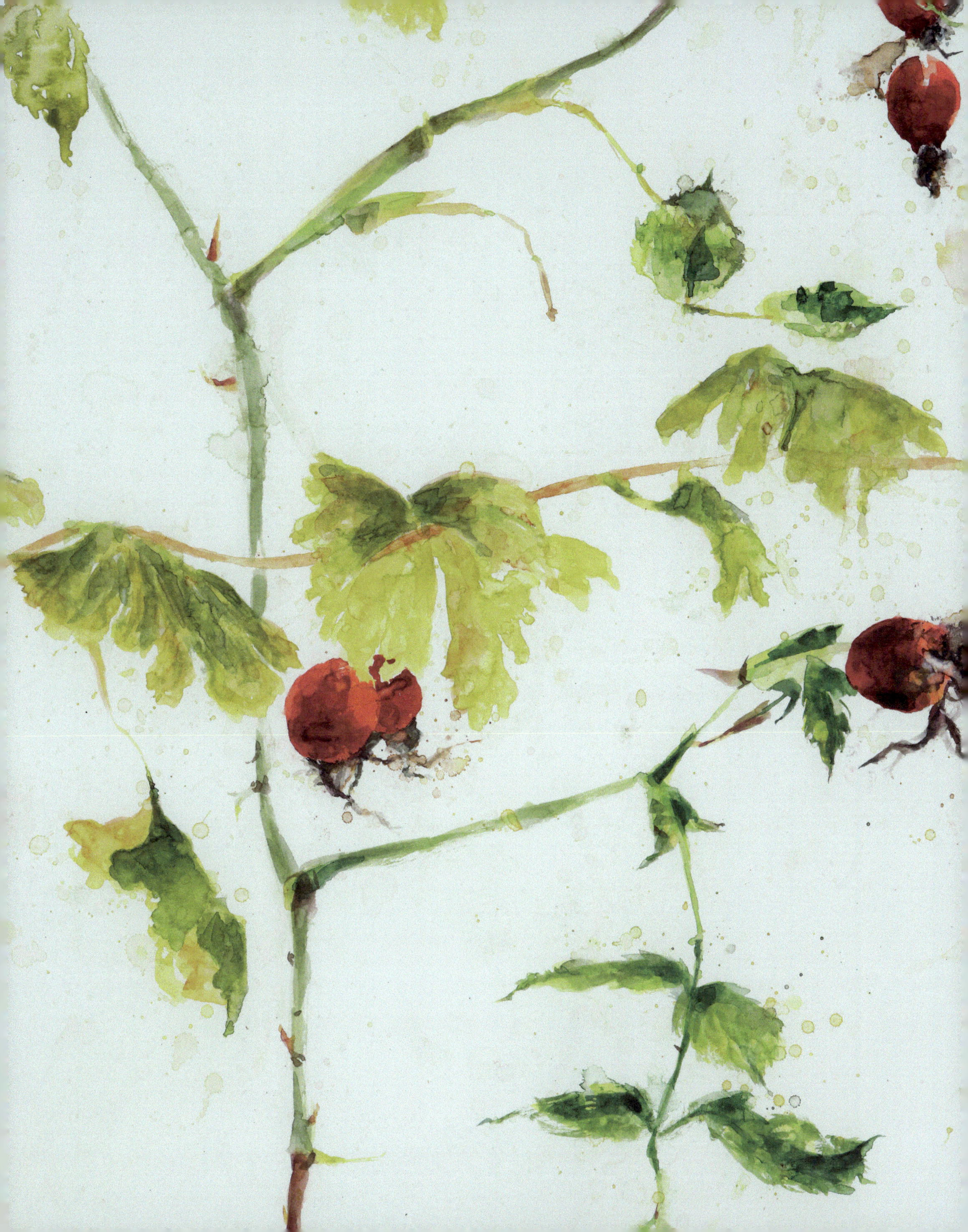

No future without fungi

They're beyond our childhood question:
animal, vegetable or mineral? Fungi, their own
myriad world, millions unexplored.

Touch them and they'll send a puff of spores
enough to change our world.
Some seem more like mineral; oyster shells
on some exotic coral. And they're mighty underground.

How old is that tree stump they've colonised?
Did they arrive last night or a century ago?
Did the moss consent to this intimate invasion?

Give us a few years and we'll be wearing them,
cured by them, cleansed by them. Meanwhile
we ask, with their spatial memory like a bee,
where are they going? How much do they know?

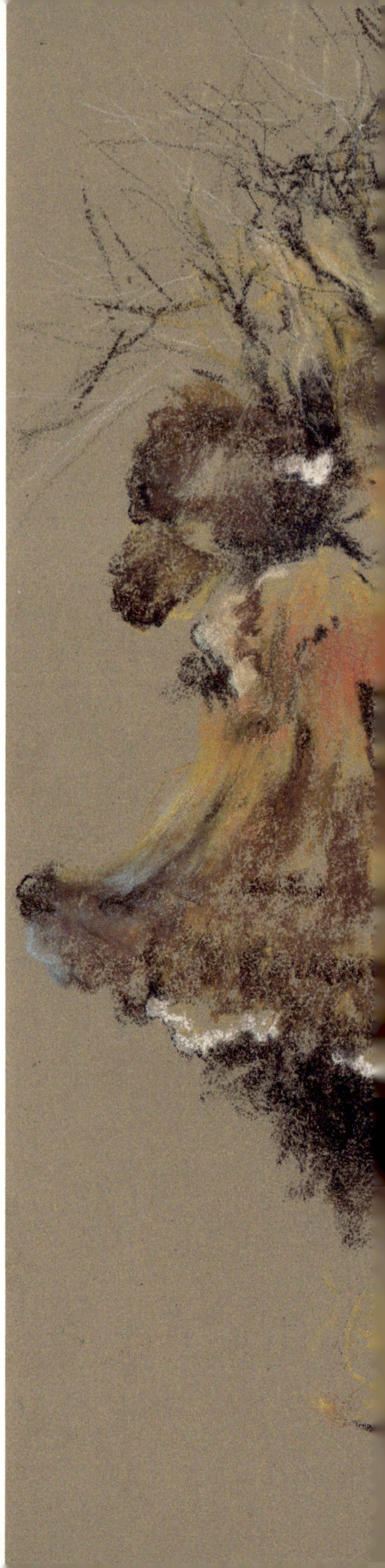

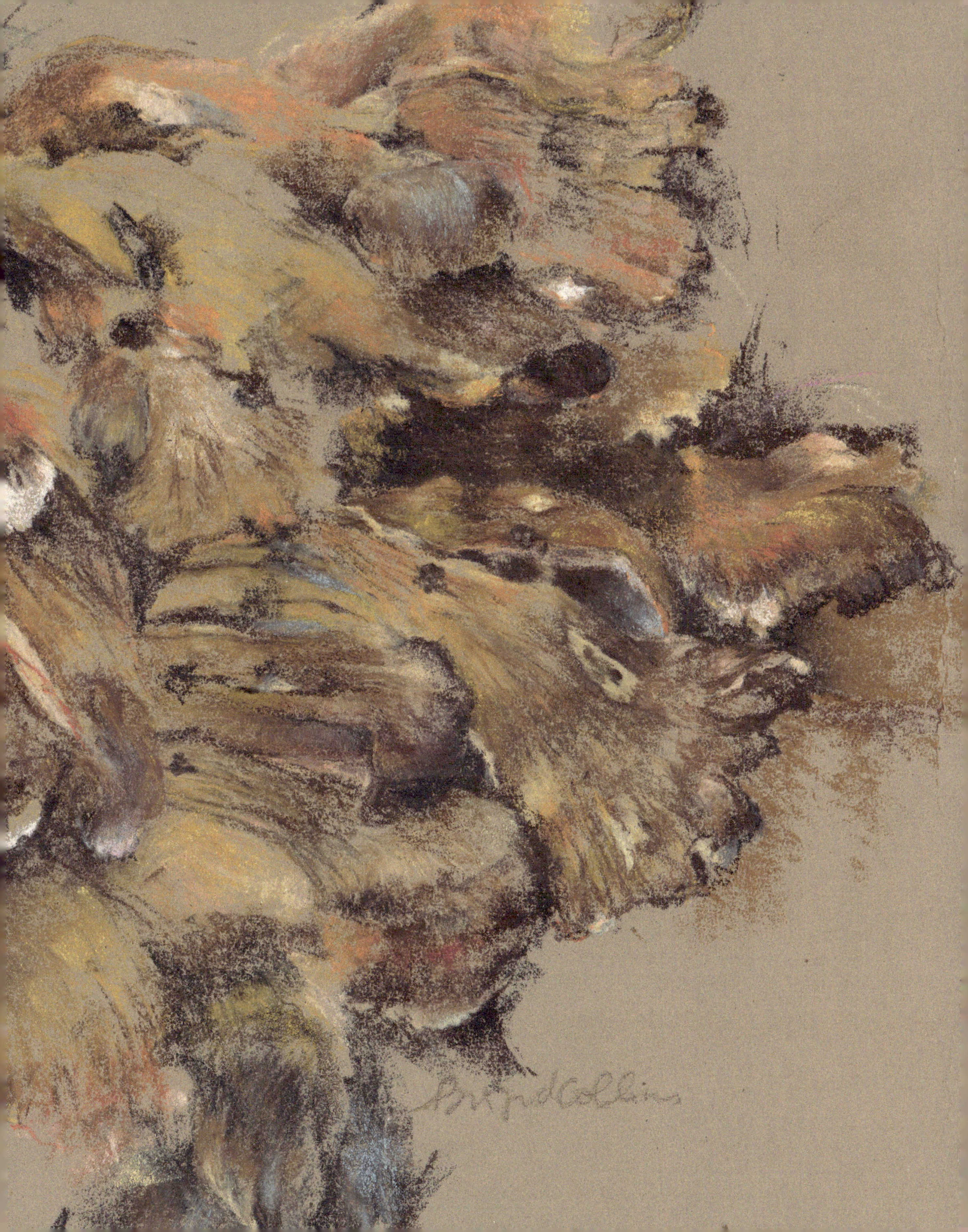

Lantern light

Grape Hyacinth – Muscari armeniacum

Your burst of cobalt
brightened Springtime,
seeds secreted deep
in the blueness of your prime.

Now you stoop and wither,
fade to modest white;
to paper lanterns hanging
like quiet temple lights.

Will the planter tap you
to gather gifts of seed,
or will they flee in a windy night?

Hold that breath till
the artist gladdens you, paints
your shadows, restores glimmers.

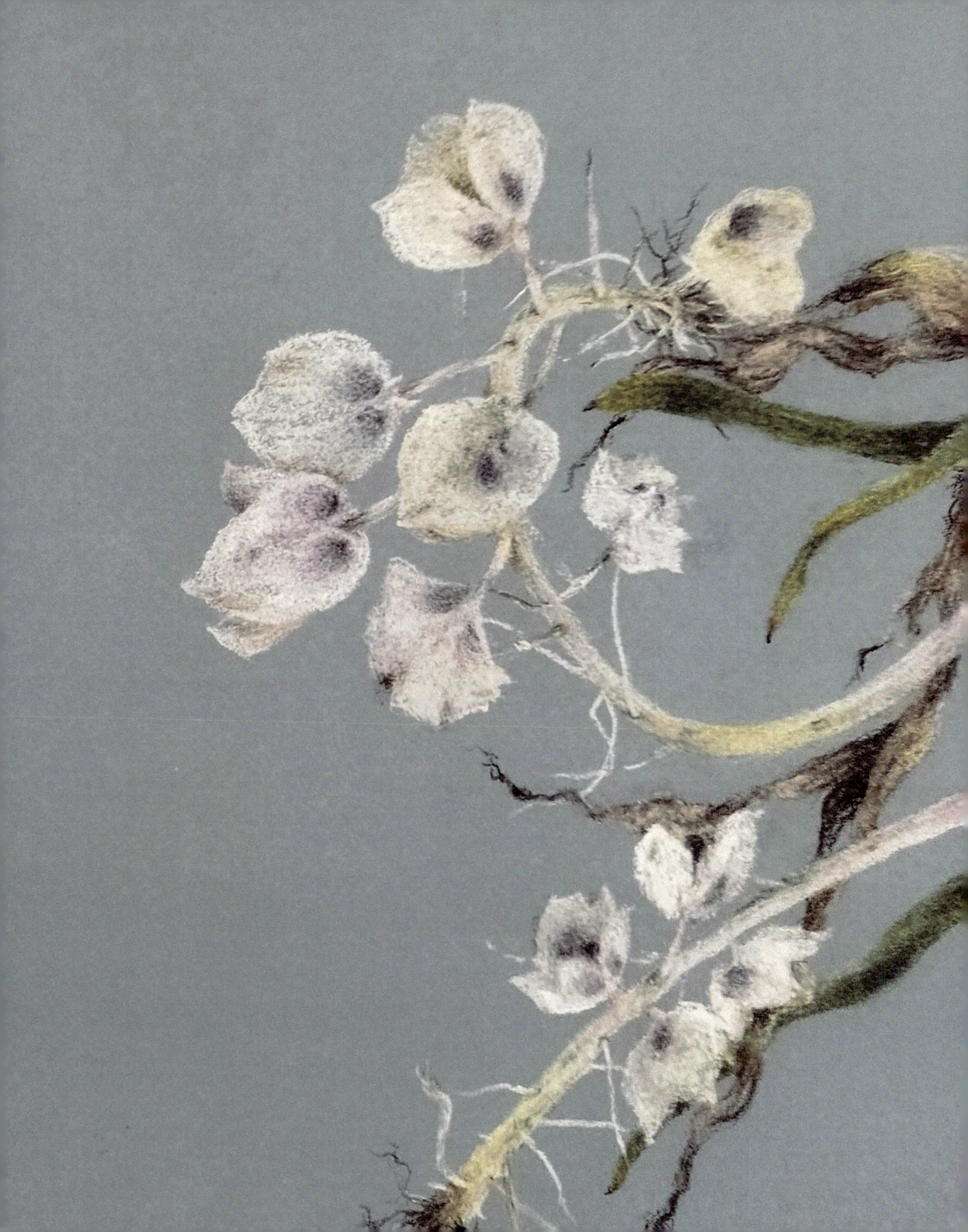

WINTER

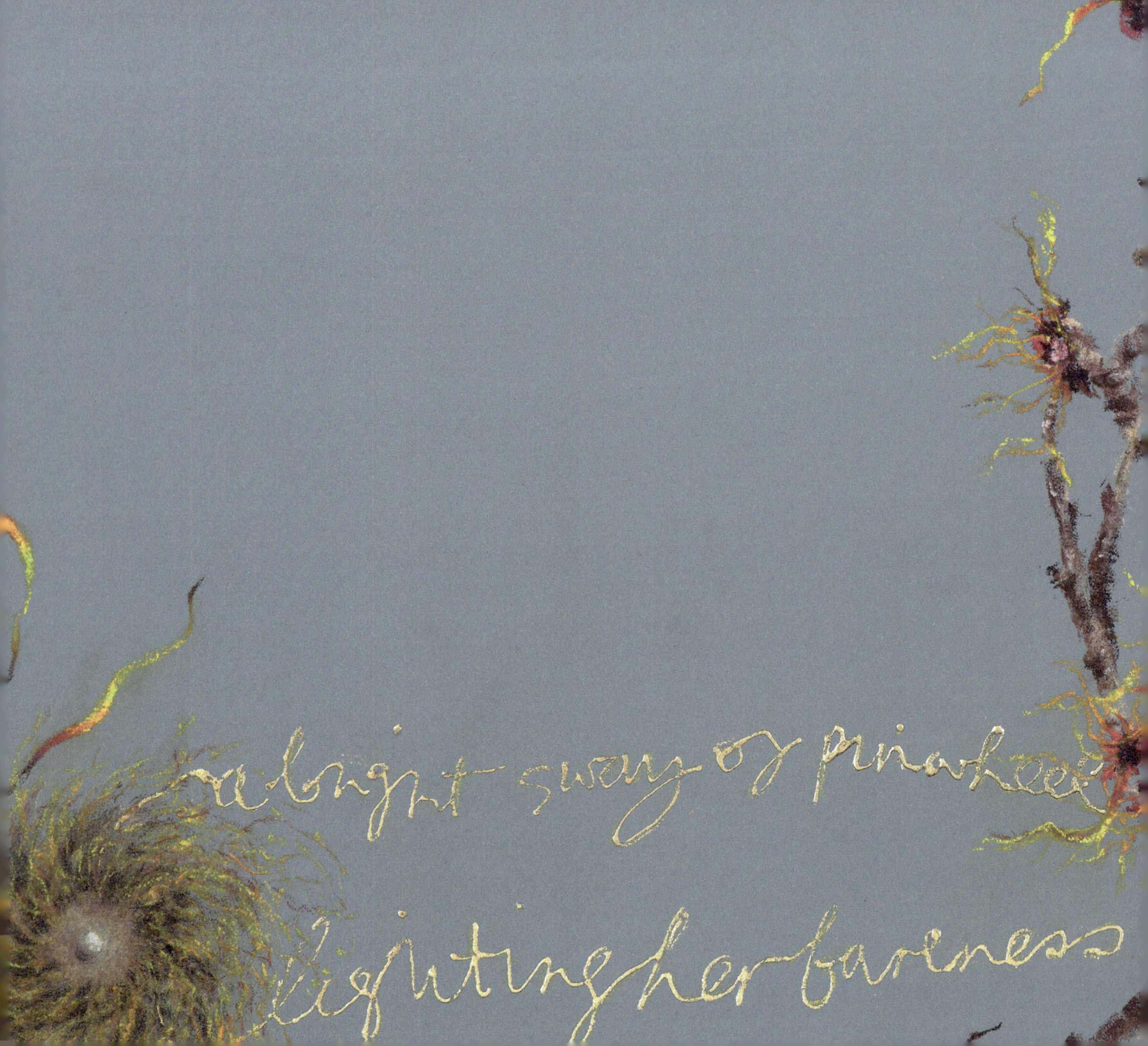

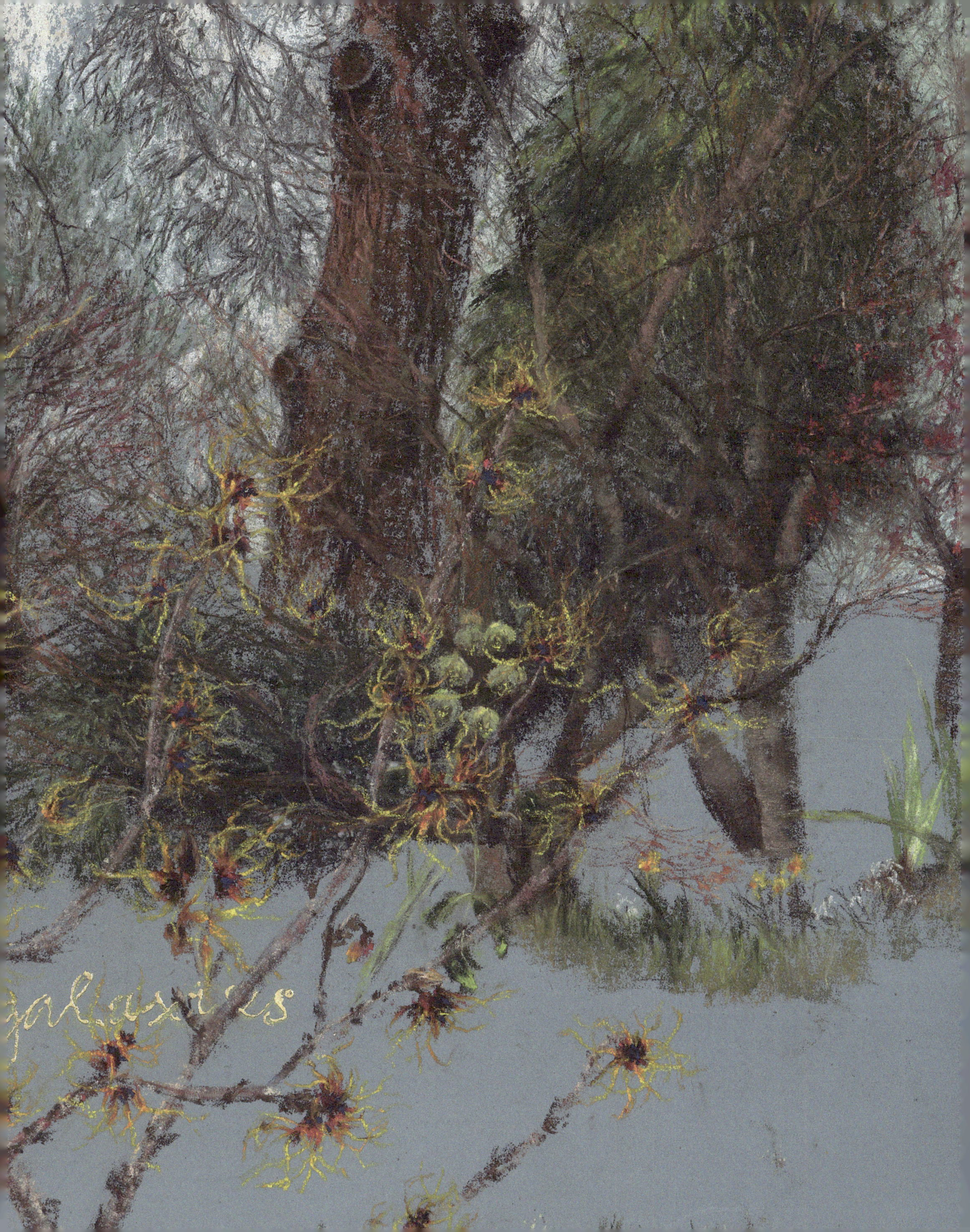
galaxies

Something of the marvellous

'In all things of nature there is something of the marvellous' —Aristotle

Mornings still nip at our heels,
kill tender shoots; but this group
are emboldened by the witch hazel:
a harbinger of warmer days,
a bright sway of pinwheel galaxies

lighting her bareness.
Might they spiral off
into new life-forms:
fireflies of the north,
glowing in the dark?

The old pine has seen it all,
the fir weathered many winters
but the delicate acer is in awe,
and the apricot offers them all
her momentary blessing.

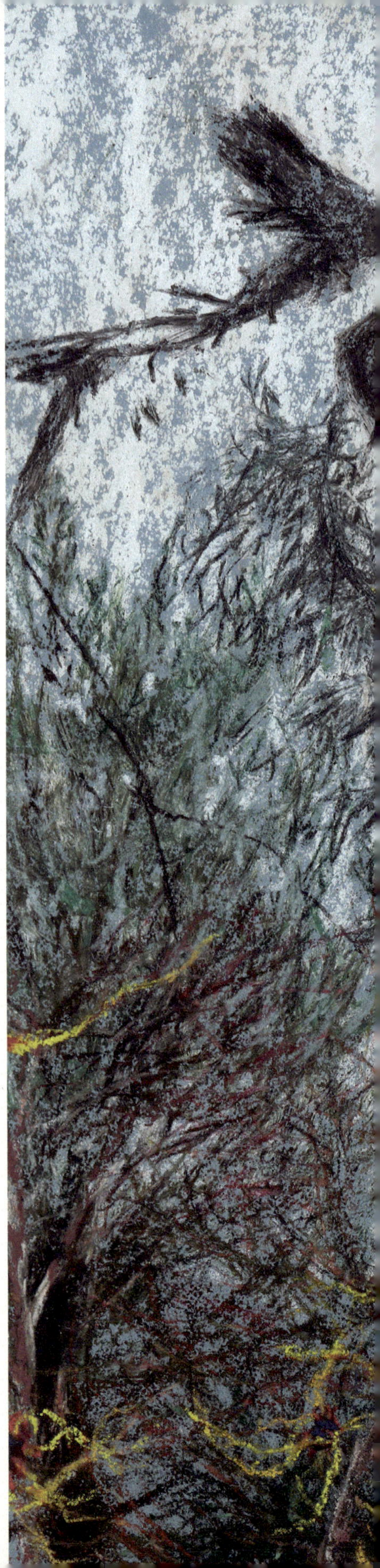

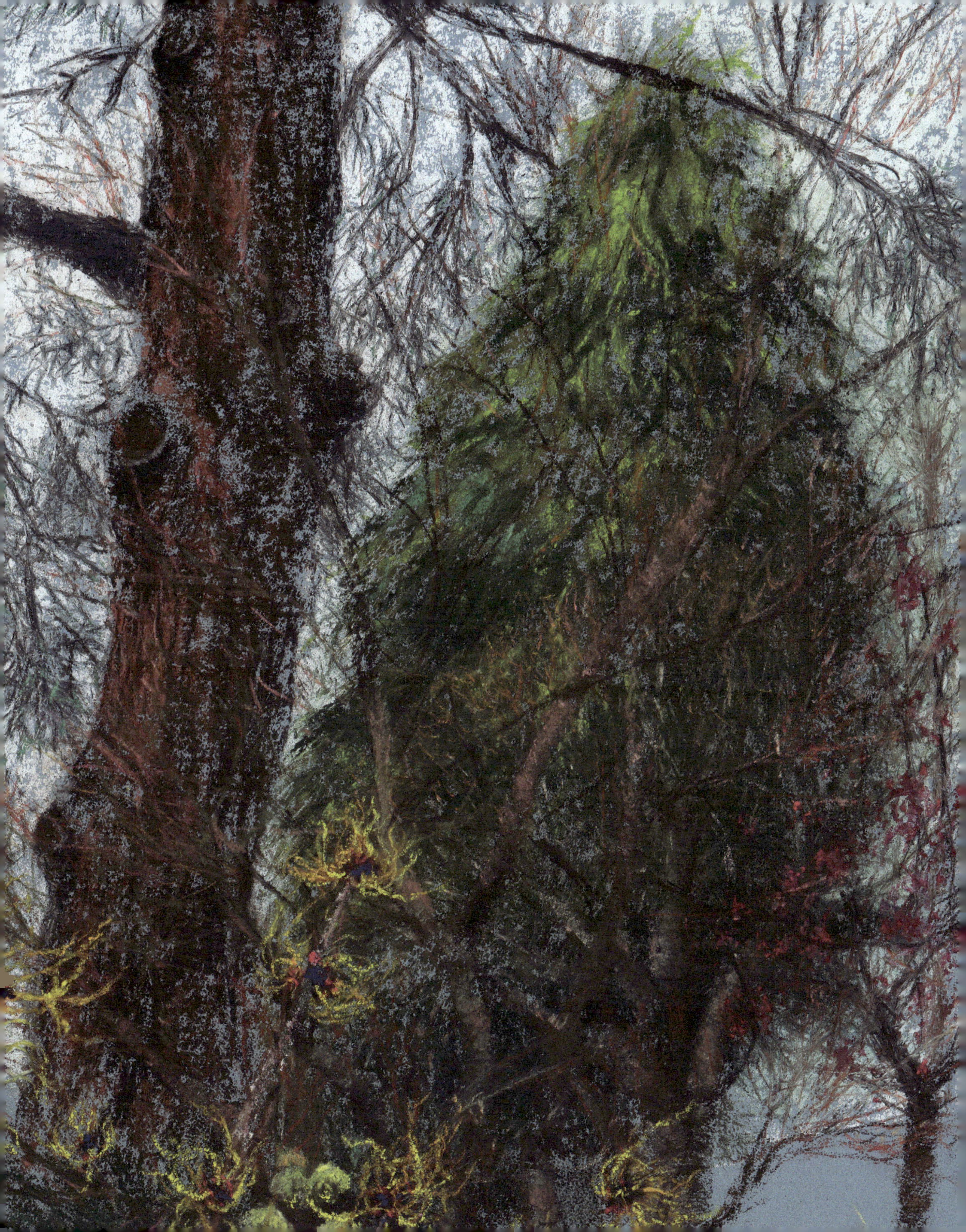

Symbols

You are drawing in the garden while
I am far away, traversing a frozen bay
fringed with reeds and pussy-willow:
I gather stems of each to savour.
Sun sinks early through chill stillness.

By the loch, you find reeds ready to cut;
and willow catkins, snug in grey fur, beg
to be stroked, to have you close.
Dogwood looks on fire, a burning bush.

In the north where palms don't thrive,
willow and rush will welcome Easter.
In the garden you weave a Brigid cross
from reeds: it will last through summer
like the velvet buds still alive in my vase.

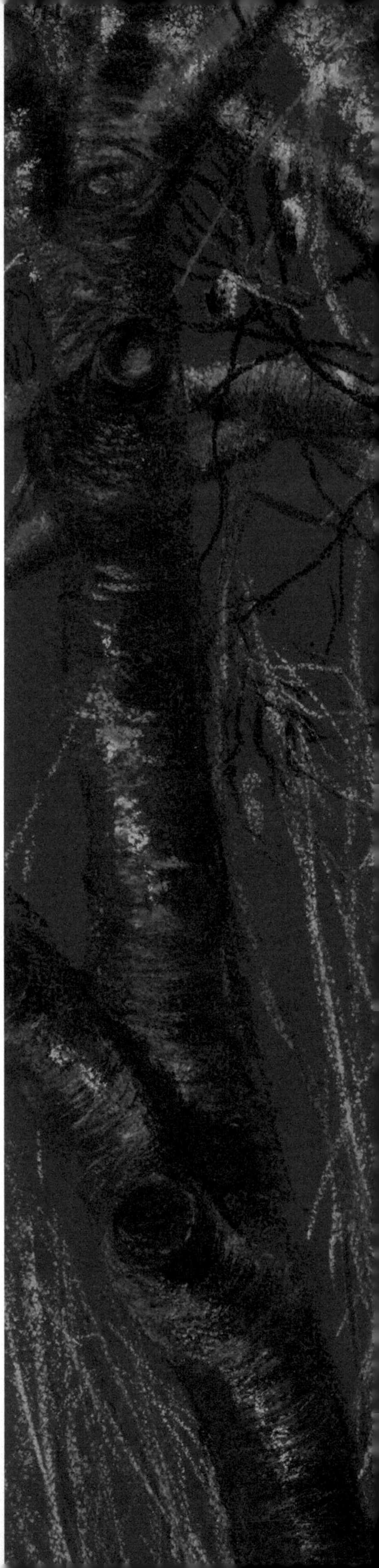

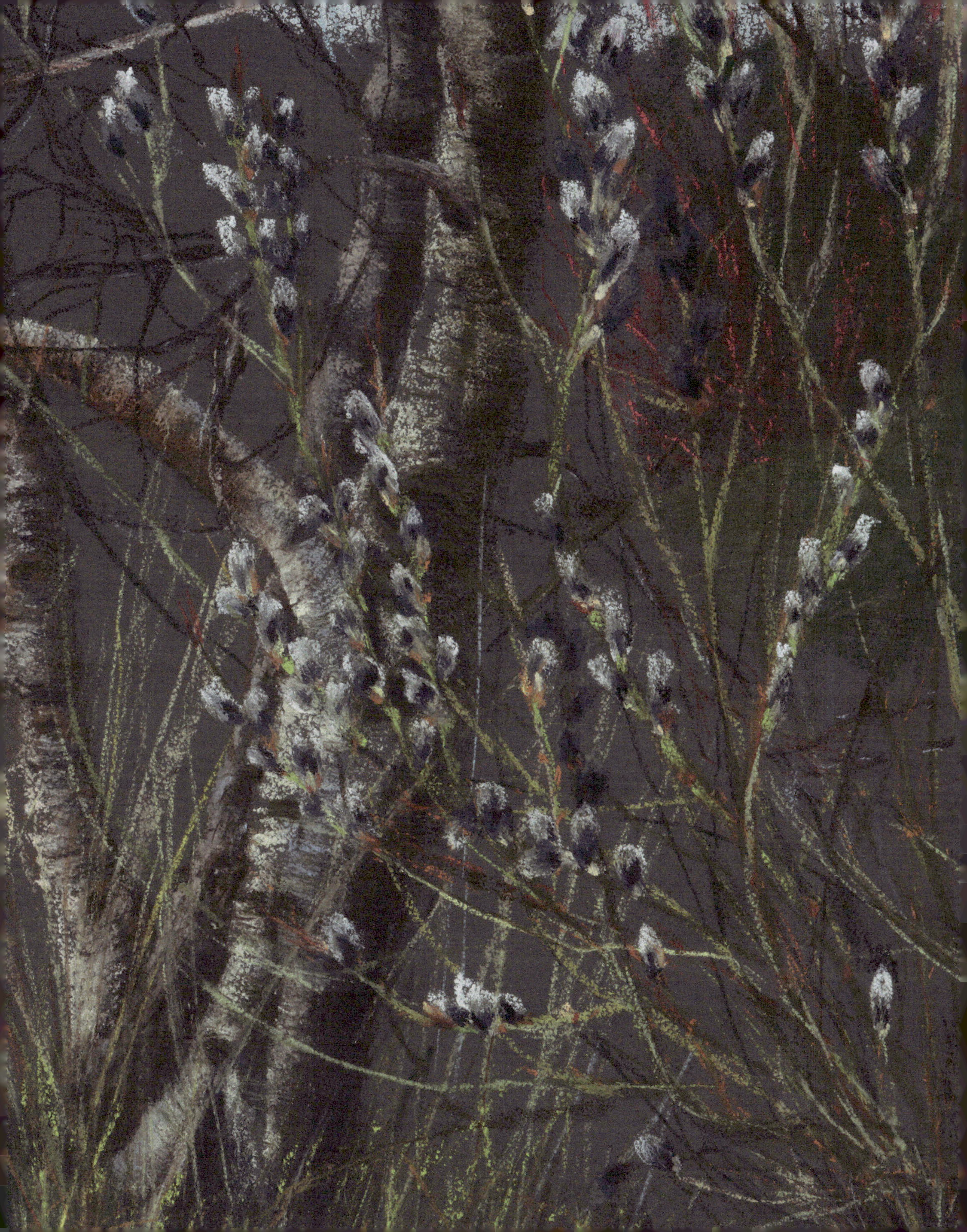

Symbiosis

Weeping birch and friends

You've been here
at the loch edge long enough
to gnarl and twist, branch out a bit.

You are hospitable
to crusty lichen gilding your branches,
to reeds that make music with you
when the wind rises.

You soothe
the solace-seeker, delight in whispering
companions, excite the dogwood
that blazes in your shade.

The cherry has lost
its calendar, paints you an early Spring.
What a picture you make
growing ever more together.

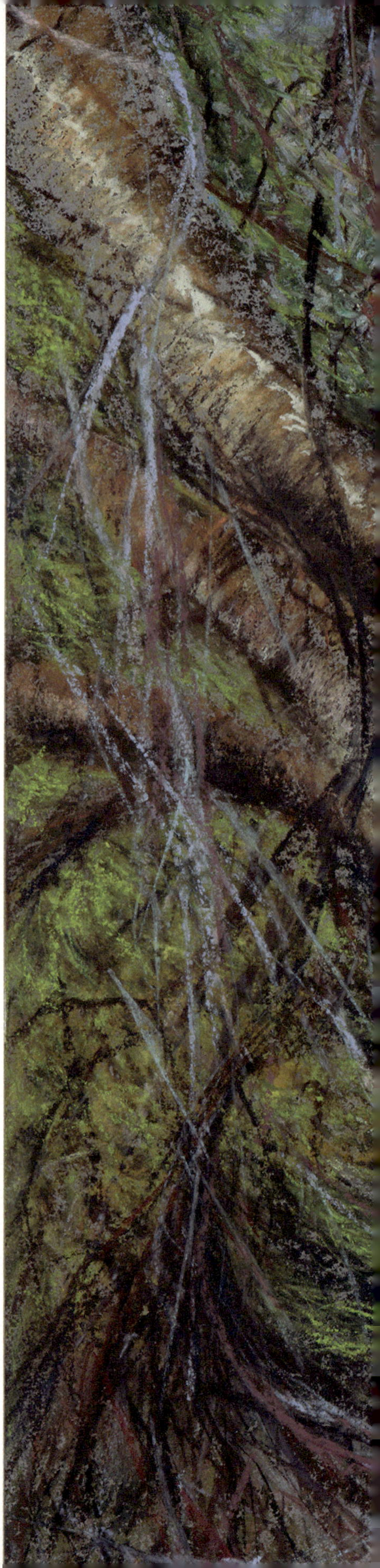

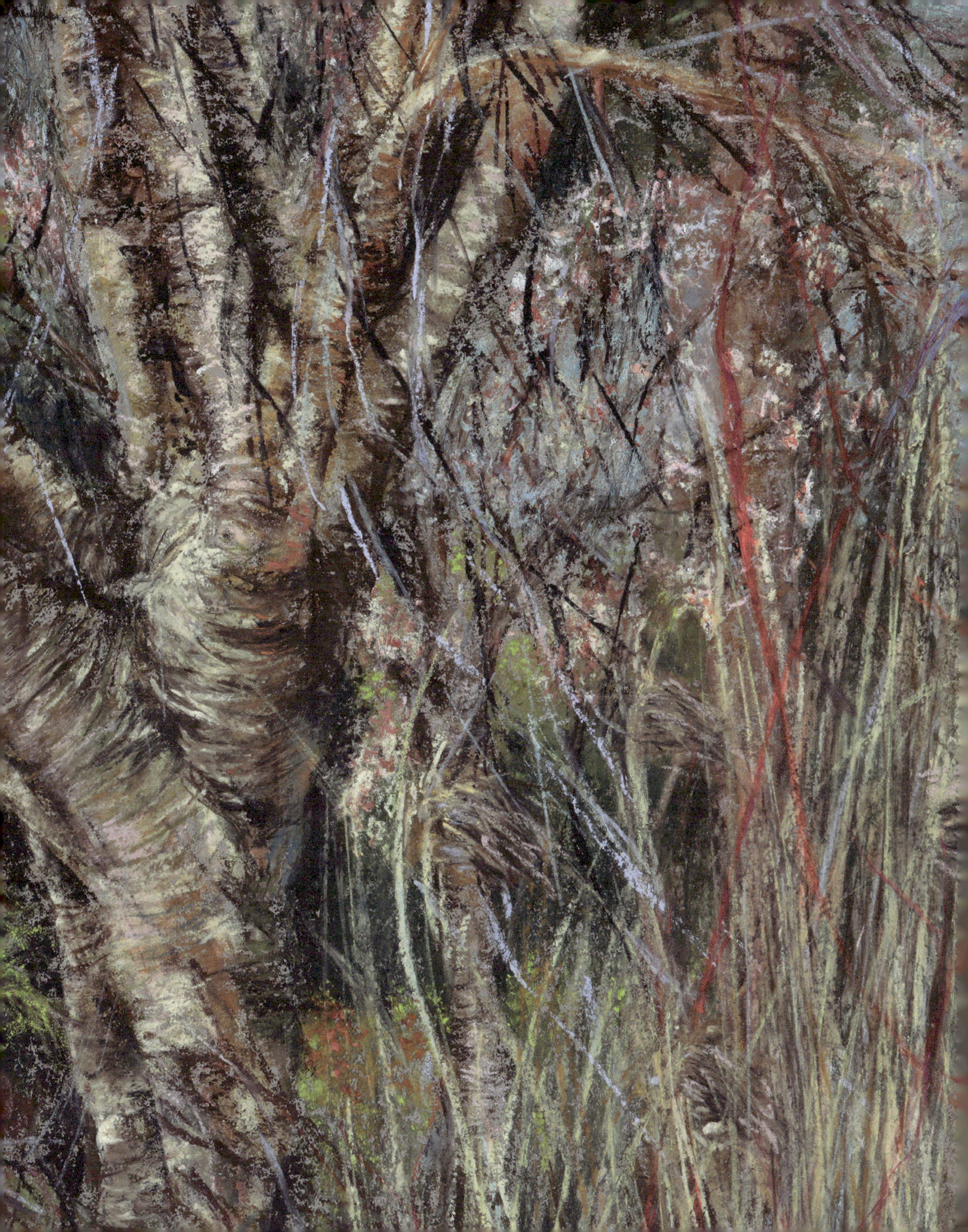

Sharing space

Chinese Red Birch

Your name is misleading or perhaps
you're keen to fit in with the locals,
not stick out like a specimen, nurtured
and exotic. Your winter trunk gives
little away; it's almost as silvered as
local birches, though there's a hint of pink.

Wind-wrapped in willow fronds, it seems
you've happily bedded in; found
your feet eased in the damp grasses,
caught their whisperings, their welcome.

In Spring you will delight them with
bright leaves and catkins; then peel back
that bark to spice up summer.

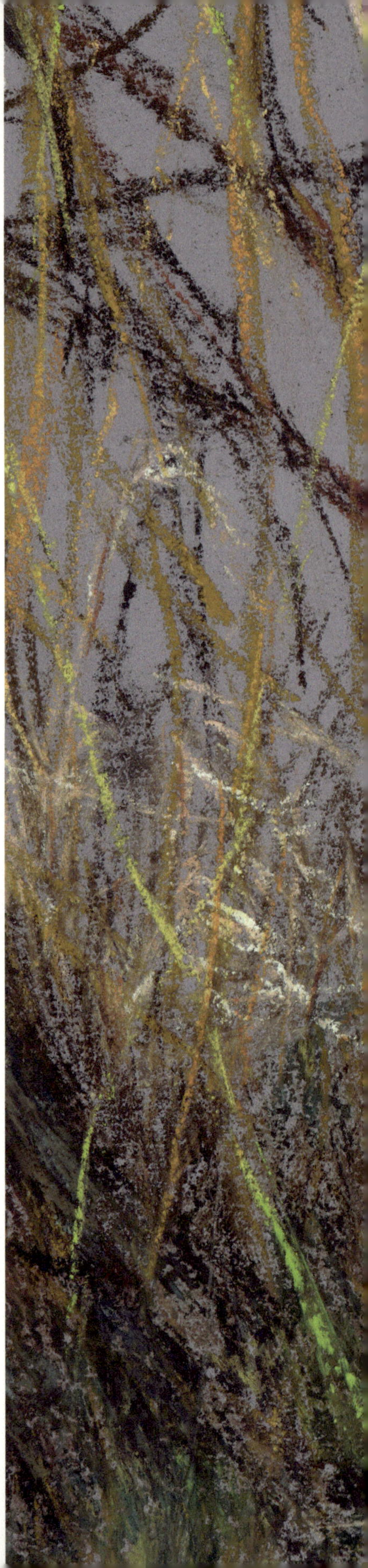

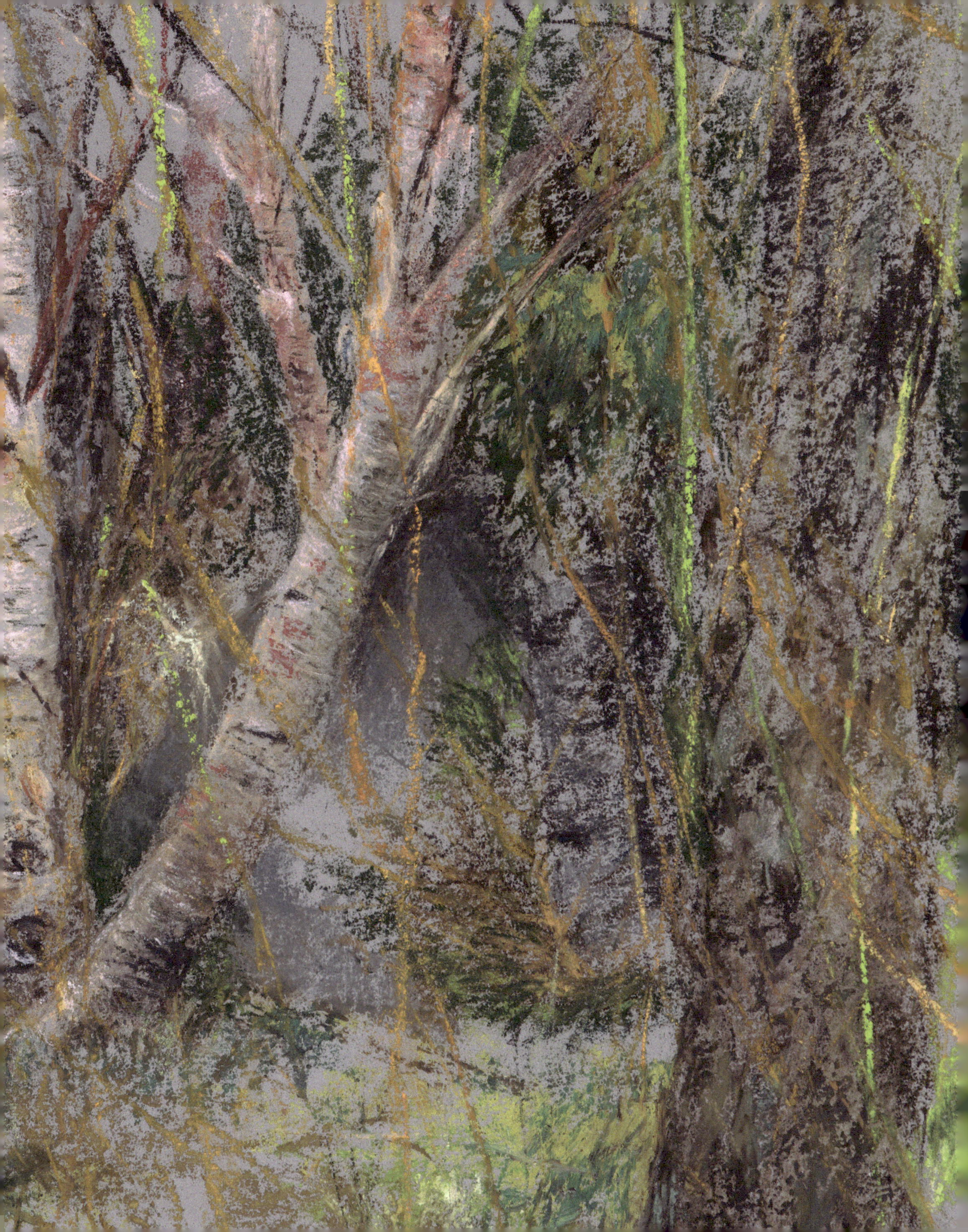

Winter gifts

Sky and loch are leached of light –
all is muted now; the sun ignites
candles on the pussy-willow.

Bullrushes are bleached.
A north wind bends the birch,
whips its stark resilient limbs.

Buds are mustering energy
one day at a time.

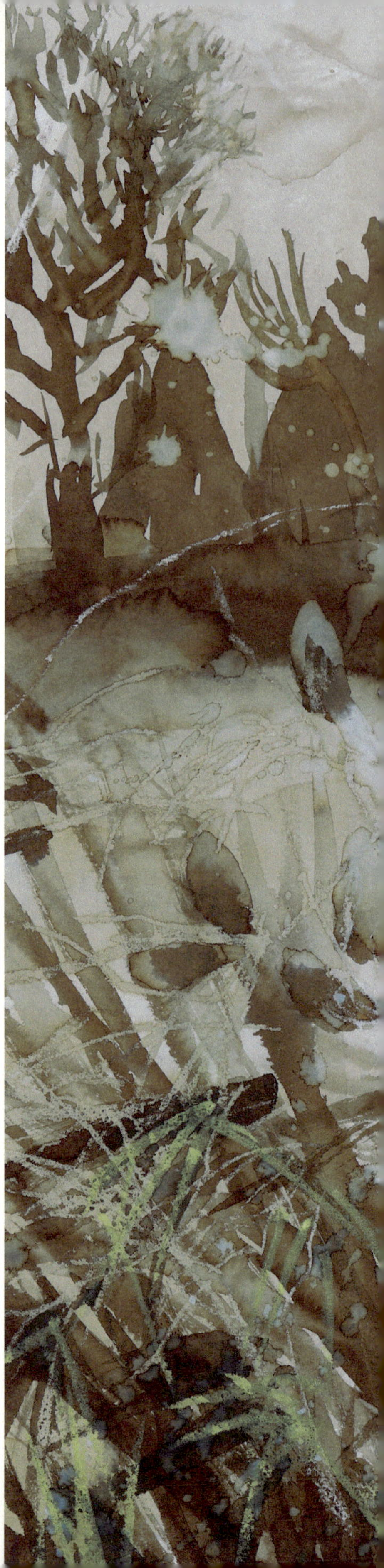

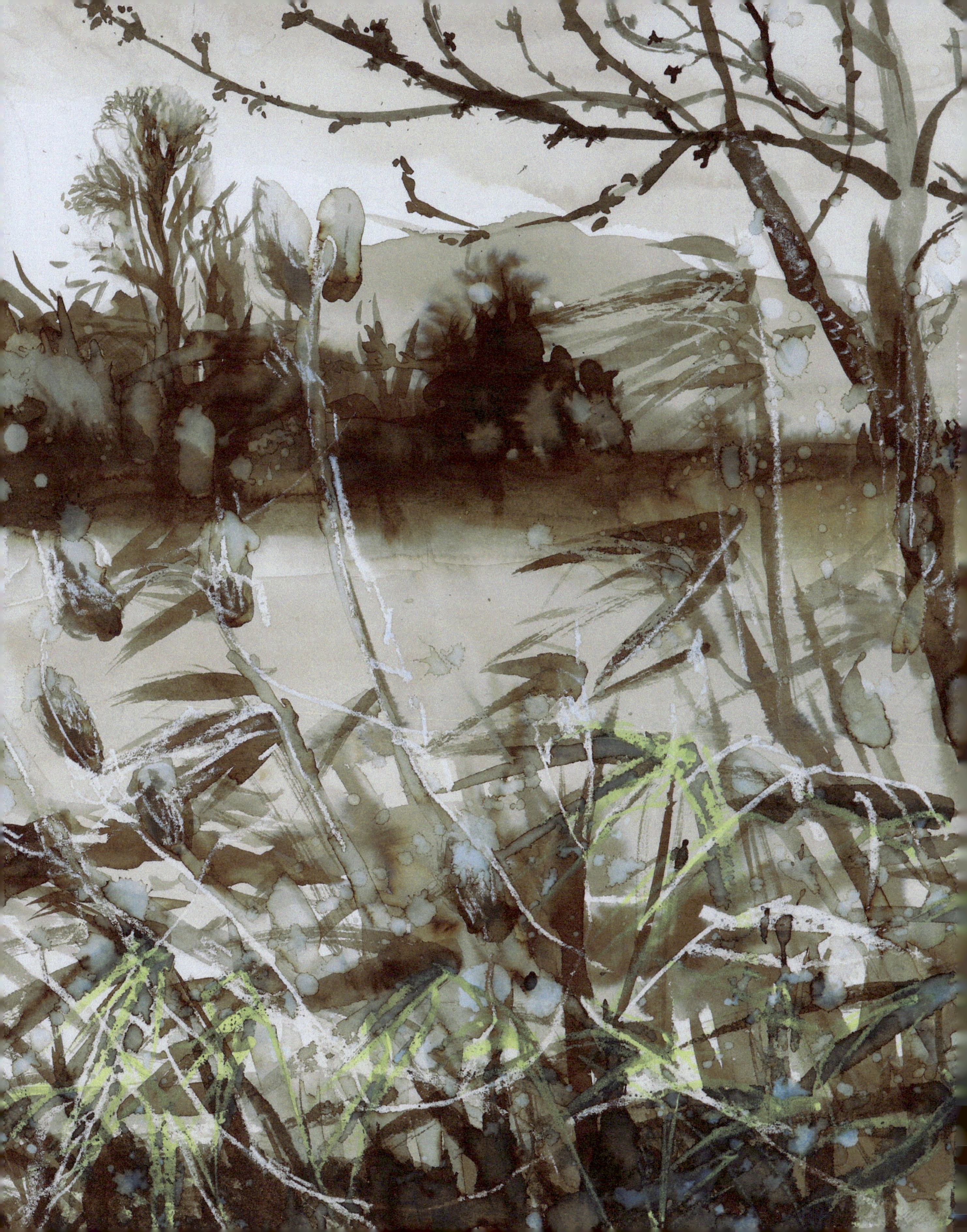

"Seeing is of course very much a matter of verbalization. Unless I call my attention to what passes before my eyes, I simple won't see it. It is, as Ruskin says, *not merely unnoticed, but in the full, clear sense of the word, unseen.* ...When I see this way I analyze and pry.

"But there is another kind of seeing that involves a letting go. When I see this way I sway transfixed and emptied. The difference between the two ways of seeing is the difference between walking with and without a camera.

"When I walk with a camera I walk from shot to shot, reading the light. When I walk without a camera, my own shutter opens, and the moment's light prints on my own silver gut. When I see this second way I am above all an unscrupulous observer..."

—From 'Seeing', an essay by Annie Dillard

"I return to my senses"

—Henry David Thoreau

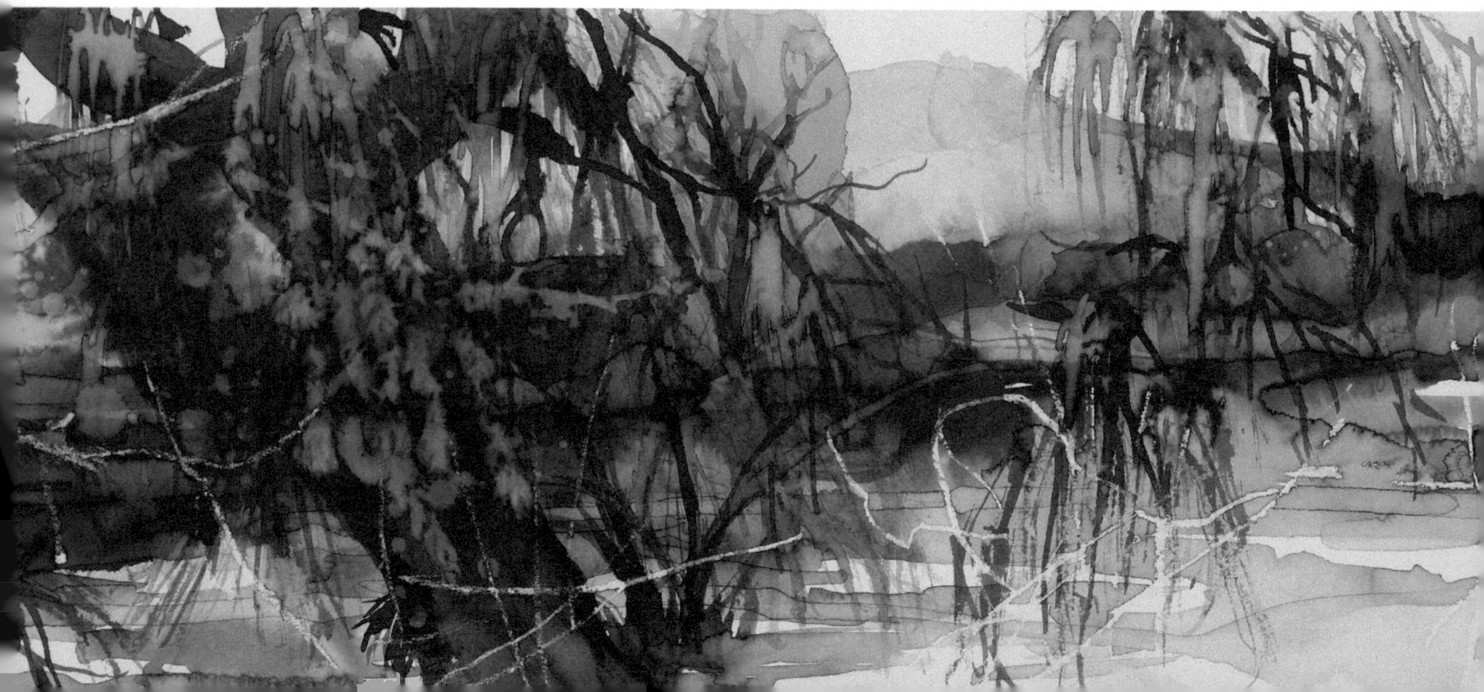

Afterword: A Special Resonance

Brigid Collins

Following a life-changing visit to Japan, which saw me spending time and drawing in Japanese gardens in Osaka, Nara, Kyoto and Matsue, a new body of work emerged through which I moved away from the type of seeing described above by American essayist and nature writer Annie Dillard – towards a deeper kind of seeing, closer to Thoreau's 'return to my senses'.

In a world in which sustained attention seems constantly under attack, eroded from without and within, paying close attention becomes more urgently necessary than ever, if we are to recover ourselves.

Absorbing influences of shodō, ink art, shakkei and 'borrowed landscape', along with kintsugi (a process of repair, made by a highlighting of flaws or breaks using gold in order to more fully understand the nature of brokenness) has brought me to a new phase in my work.

That it began *en plein air* became even more significant, as weather and the elements played their part while I drew and painted in Dr Neil's Garden. During time spent there as Artist in Residence, consciously sheltering in this magical setting following much loss, I came to notice a deepening of my creative process.

Working closely with Christine De Luca in a spirit of mutual responsiveness brought a very special synergy and resonance.

Taking form as a series of drawings, each made into a unique Artist's Book form, this new body of work included a series of larger drawings, all of which, when viewed together, form a panorama – though not a perfect one – articulating the delicate edges of the garden as they meet the surrounding landscape, both near and far ('borrowed'). A seemingly small space thus opens towards the vastness, to its utopian potential.

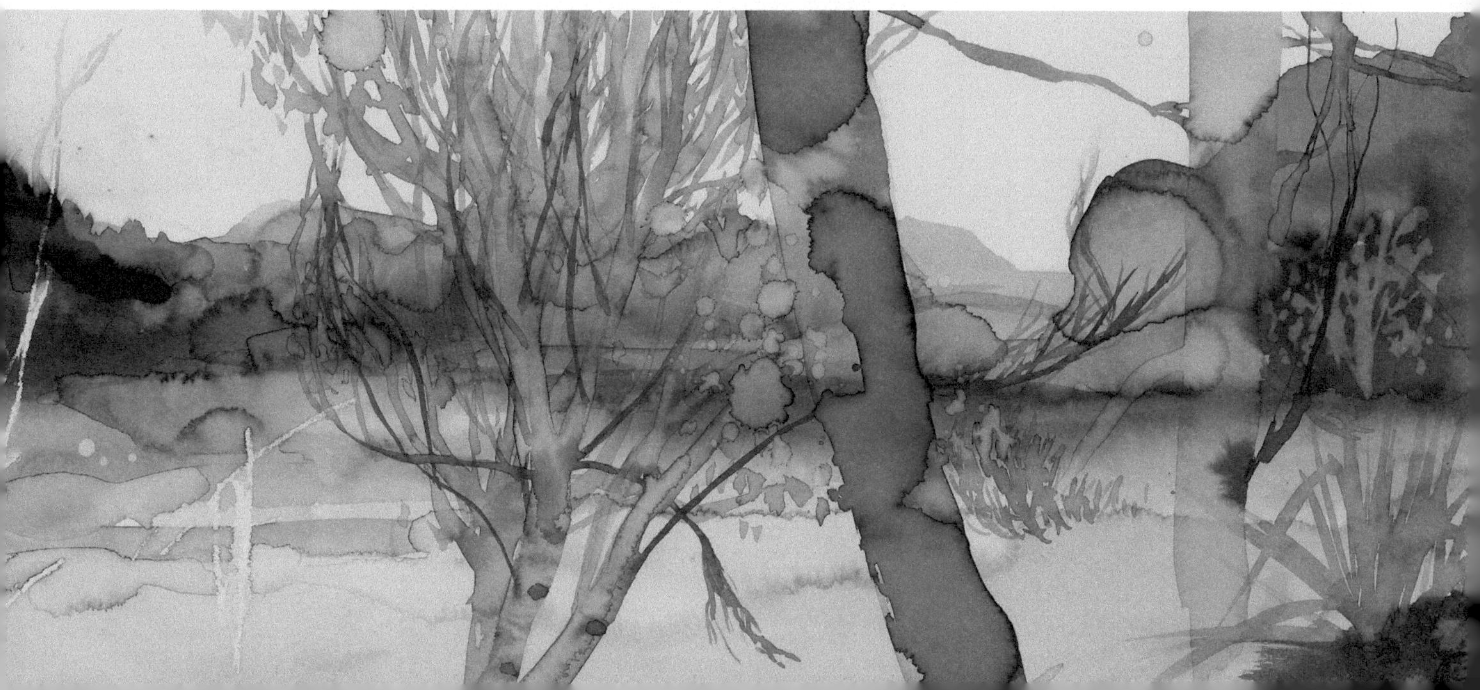

Labelling

In the beginning was the word:
that capture of thought, delight
in imagination, in pinning down.
We can't seem to stop ourselves
bonding memories to words;
language to help recall the moment.

The baby touches, we say the word;
he points again, babbles, we repeat
and sound it out till he says it
the way we say it. Now he holds
the magic for himself.

We learn to love what
we attend to, what we label.
But memory can falter, is prone
to gaps and lapses. We rummage
for a word, a name, a thought;

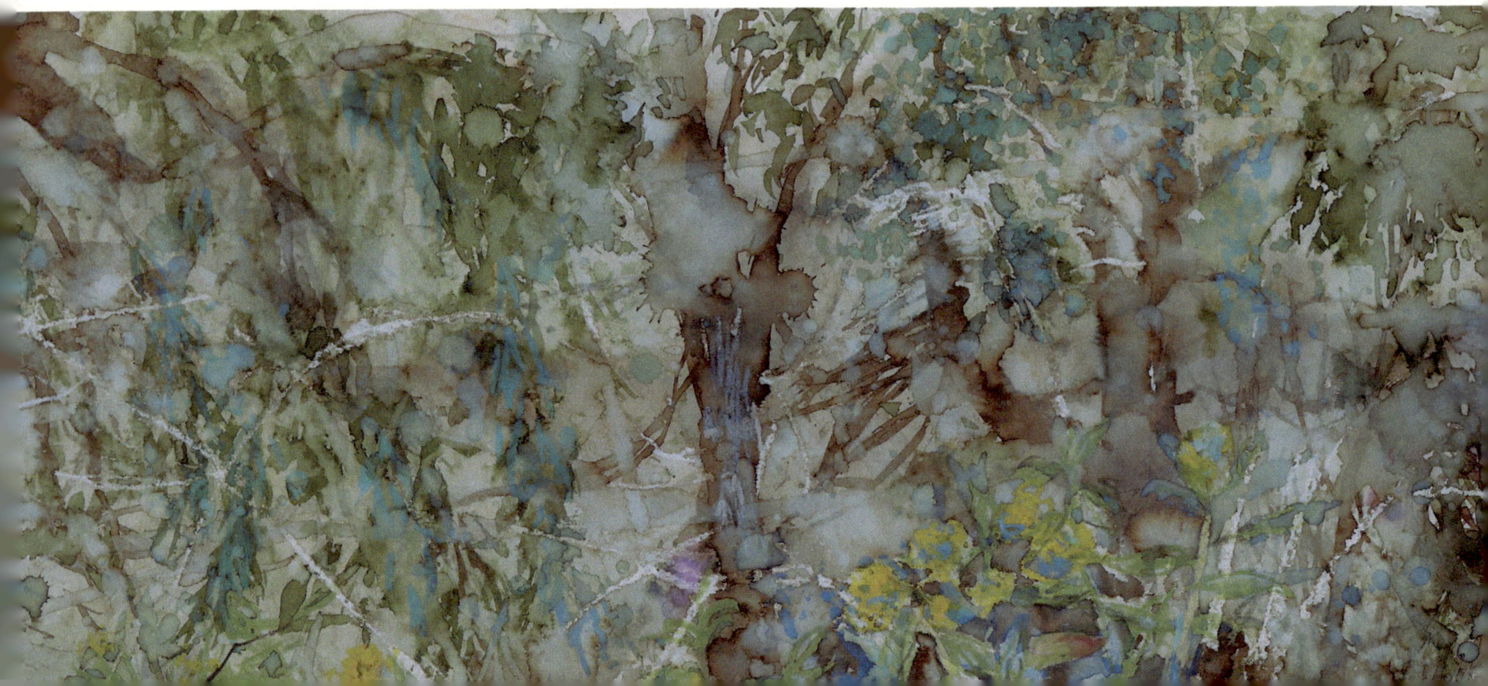

can find ourselves back to
the simplicity of the unnamed,
attending to each other:
just me and that little brown bird
whose legs the sun makes almost
see-through, showering in the bird-bath.

Words can tumble away from us,
as if released, exposing sentience.
Is it that rose that we smell? Love is
at the beginning and at the end.

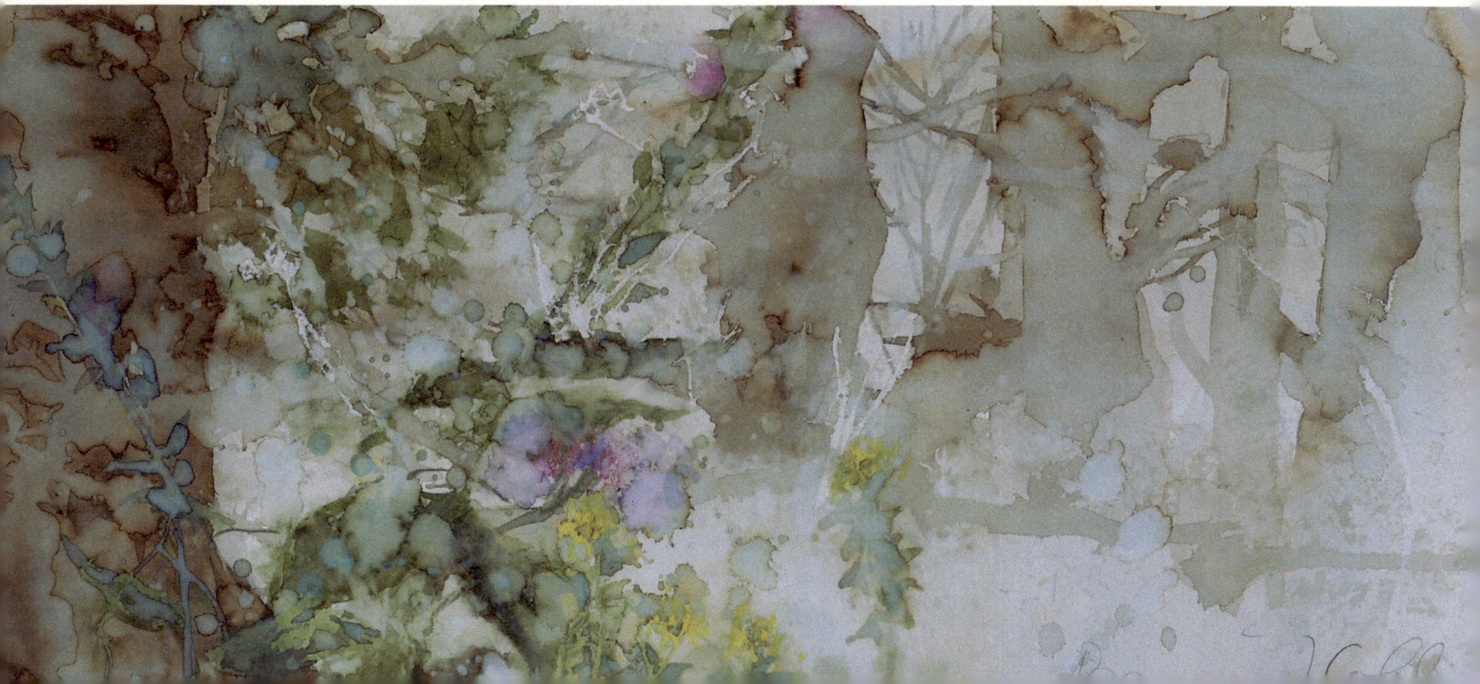

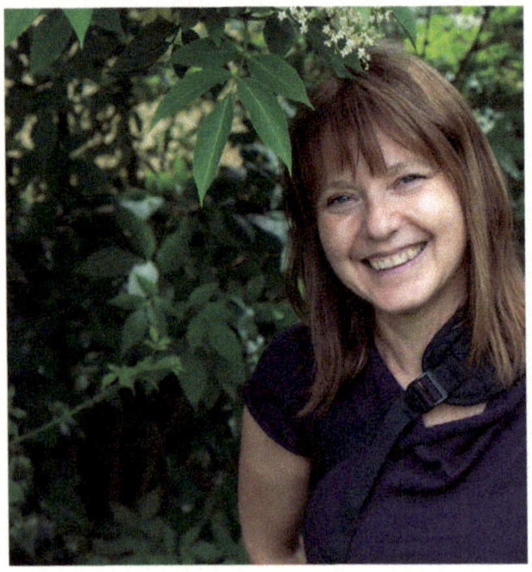

Brigid Collins

Brigid is an artist and educator whose practice is deeply rooted in close and loving observation of the natural world. She makes paintings and drawings inspired by poetry as well as working in three dimensions and with the form of the book. She is most often drawn to the tactility and sensuousness of materials such as pastels, watercolour, porcelain, tissue, wire and wax, encapsulating fragility and strength in equal measure. She has collaborated and published books with poets and authors Seamus Heaney, Kathleen Jamie and Kirsty Gunn and, most recently, also with poet Christine De Luca. The collaboration with Christine was undertaken while spending a year as Artist in Residence at Dr Neil's Garden in Duddingston, Edinburgh, where artworks, poems and a short film which resulted from their collaboration were exhibited at Midsummer in Playfair's wonderful Thomson's Tower, set deep in the garden on the shores of the Duddingston Loch.

Having just spent such a very happy and healing time working almost exclusively outdoors, Brigid is currently focusing on developing new work and hopes to begin to find ways to build on this practice of working *en plein air*.

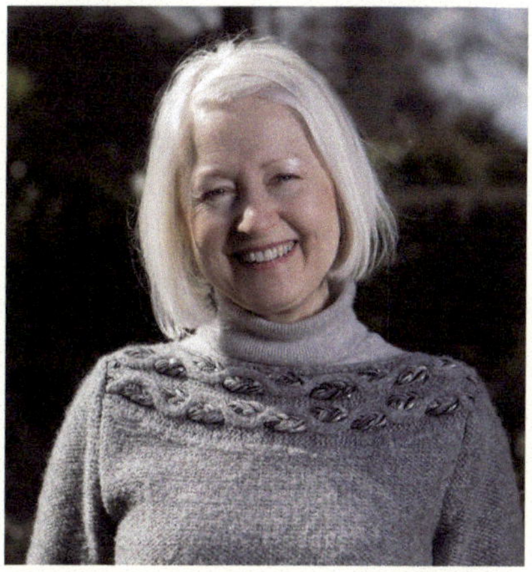

Christine De Luca

Christine writes in English and Shaetlan (Shetlandic), her mother tongue. She was appointed Edinburgh's Makar (laureate) for 2014–2017. She has had eight poetry collections published, several of which have won awards. She has also written two novels and several storybooks for children. She particularly enjoys collaborating with artists and musicians. *Another Time, Another Place* (The Scottish Gallery, 2021) documented a collaboration with the Scottish artist, Victoria Crowe. Her poetry has inspired both jazz and classical compositions, most recently collaborating with Tommy Smith and Orkney-based composer Gemma McGregor.

She is also active in translation, with six bilingual poetry collections published as well as a few classic storybooks for children.

Acknowledgements & Credits

Introduction

Page 9:
Quote from *Vesper Flights* by Helen MacDonald (Jonathan Cape 2020)

Quote from Rowan Williams, from a talk given at New College Festival of Books and Religion (2022)

Quote from *How To See Nature* by Paul Evans (Batsford 2018)

Quote from the late Thich Nhat Hanh, Buddhist monk

Quote from Mary Oliver, poet, in *Upstream* by Mary Oliver (UK: Penguin, 2016)

Page 10:
Quote from Brian Eno, from Brian Eno's Facebook page (01-08-2022)

Page 11:
Quote from 'Where birds felt louder: The garden as a refuge during COVID-19', in *Wellbeing, Space and Society*, Volume 2, 2021

Extract from *Meditations* by Dr Kitty Wheater, Mindfulness Chaplain and Associate of the Global Compassion Institute at the University of Edinburgh, made possible with the kind support of 'Art and Spiritual Understanding', a research project with the School of Divinity at The University of Edinburgh, funded by Templeton Religion Trust.

Dr Neil's Garden

Page 13:
Extract from 'Where birds felt louder: The garden as a refuge during COVID-19', in *Wellbeing, Space and Society*, Volume 2, 2021

Afterword

Page 62:
Extract from 'Seeing', an essay by Annie Dillard, *Pilgrim at Tinker Creek* (HarperCollins USA, 1974: Canterbury Press, UK, 2011)

Poems

'Lull'
'Hark, what peaceful music rings.'
from *Jesu, joy of man's desiring*, by J S Bach, translated by Robert Bridges

'Something of the Marvellous'
'In all things of nature there is something of the marvellous.'
from *De Partibus Animalium* – book 1, by Aristotle

Photography Credits

Sue Stuart-Smith (www.suestuartsmith.com)
Brigid Collins by David R Moss
Christine De Luca by Dawn Marie Jones
Brigid and Christine in the garden by Nico Kumar
Brigid's artworks photographed by A&M Imaging, Edinburgh
Claudia Pottier and Jane Garven by Beth Mollison

Design

Tim Bremner – initial design concept
Typesetting – Main Point Books

Websites

Brigid Collins https://suchfragilefutures.brigidcollinsart.com/
Christine De Luca www.christinedeluca.co.uk
Main Point Books www.mainpointbooks.co.uk
Tim Bremner bremnerdesign.co.uk
Dr. Neil's Garden https://www.drneilsgarden.co.uk/

Thanks

This book could not have happened without the unwavering support of the then-gardener at Dr Neil's Garden, Claudia Pottier and of the volunteers, who continue to bring so much joy and mutual support throughout each day that we spend in this special place.

Much gratitude also must be extended to Carol and her crew in the Garden Room Café and to all at Dr Neil's Garden Trust. The garden would, of course, not exist were it not for the work and vision of Drs Nancy and Andrew Neil, who created it from a wilderness. Their work is now being continued by the current gardener, Alan Mitchell.

We are also deeply grateful for the interest, support and friendship shown to us and our work by Dr Sue Stuart-Smith, author of the best-selling and incredibly wise book *The Well-Gardened Mind*, who has so graciously written the Foreword to this book.

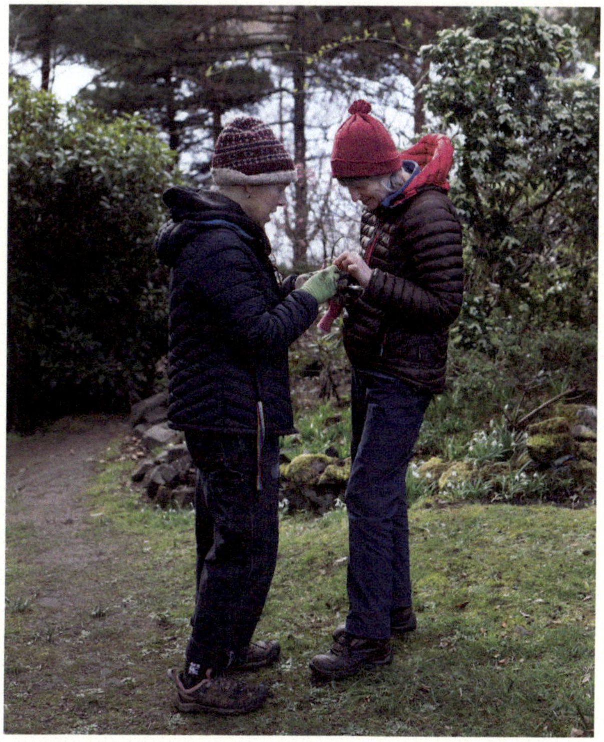

(Right: Claudia Pottier and Jane Garven in Dr Neil's Garden.)